When I Grow Up

I CAN BE A SINGER

By Alex Appleby

Gareth Stevens
PUBLISHING

Please visit our website, www.garethstevens.com. For a free color catalog of all our high-quality books, call toll free 1-800-542-2595 or fax 1-877-542-2596.

Library of Congress Cataloging-in-Publication Data

Appleby, Alex.
I can be a singer / by Alex Appleby.
p. cm. — (When I grow up)
Includes index.
ISBN 978-1-4824-0758-7 (pbk.)
ISBN 978-1-4824-1006-8 (6-pack)
ISBN 978-1-4824-0757-0 (library binding)
1. Singers — Juvenile literature. 2. Singing — Juvenile literature. 3. Occupations — Juvenile literature. I. Appleby, Alex. II. Title.
ML3930.A2 A66 2015
784—d23

First Edition

Published in 2015 by
Gareth Stevens Publishing
111 East 14th Street, Suite 349
New York, NY 10003

Copyright © 2015 Gareth Stevens Publishing

Editor: Ryan Nagelhout
Designer: Sarah Liddell

Photo credits: Cover, p. 1 (singer) paulaphoto/Shutterstock.com; cover, p. 1 (stage) alphaspirit/Shutterstock.com; p. 5 Donald P Oehman/Shutterstock.com; p. 7 Sergey Novikov/Shutterstock.com; p. 9 Adam Taylor/Digital Vision/Thinkstock.com; p. 11 Antonio_Diaz/iStock/Thinkstock.com; p. 13 JGI/Jamie Grill/Blend Images/Getty Images; p. 15 Digital Vision/Digital Vision/Thinkstock.com; pp. 17, 24 (teacher) Christopher Futcher/Vetta/Getty Images; pp. 19, 23, Ned Frisk/Blend Images/Thinkstock.com; pp. 21, 24 (drums) Ned Frisk/Blend Images/Getty Images.

All rights reserved. No part of this book may be reproduced in any form without permission in writing from the publisher, except by a reviewer.

Printed in the United States of America

CPSIA compliance information: Batch #CS15GS: For further information contact Gareth Stevens, New York, New York at 1-800-542-2595.

Contents

Sing It! 4

School Singing. 12

The Band 22

Words to Know 24

Index. 24

I love to sing.

5

I have a great voice.

I want to be a singer when I grow up.

9

I know a lot of songs.

11

I like to sing at school.

13

I take many music classes.

15

I have a great teacher.
She is called
a voice coach.

17

I sing with my friends.

19

My friend Jane
plays the drums.

21

We have a band!

23

Words to Know

drums

teacher

Index

band 22

music classes 14

voice 6

voice coach 16

Thomas, Edith Lovell
The whole world s[inging]
by Edith Lovell Th[omas]
Kathleen Voute. --
Friendship Press, c1950.
122 p. : ill. ; 26 cm.

For voice and

Y0-CKI-109

3 1192 00228 3552

POCK   770319
8028077

M782.42083 Whole

The whole world singing / compiled by Edith Lovell Thomas. c1950.

AUG. 18 1979
SEP 1 8 1980
NOV 19 '80
JUN 1 5 1981
MAR 6 1982
MAR 2 7 1982
NOV 1 1984
APR 5 1989
DEC 2 3 1989

Evanston Public Library
Evanston, Illinois

Each reader is responsible for all books or other materials taken on his card, and for any fines or fees charged for overdues, damages, or loss.

DEMCO

SONGBOOKS FOR CHILDREN
EDITED BY EDITH LOVELL THOMAS

SINGING WORSHIP WITH BOYS AND GIRLS
SING, CHILDREN, SING
(Abingdon-Cokesbury Press)

MARTIN AND JUDY SONGS
(Beacon Press)

THE WHOLE WORLD SINGING

Compiled by
EDITH LOVELL THOMAS

drawings by
KATHLEEN VOUTE

*All are comrades, friends and brothers
In the fellowship of song.*

FRIENDSHIP PRESS
NEW YORK

ACKNOWLEDGMENTS

Appreciation is expressed to the many people in many countries whose contributions helped to make this book possible.

Grateful acknowledgment is given to Loretta Kruszyna, Assistant Editor of Children's Publications of Friendship Press, for careful work done in handling the permissions and the other multitudinous details involved in bringing out this songbook.

Thanks are extended to Paul Allwardt for thoughtful reading of manuscript and proofs.

Credit is due the following for permission to quote:

Mrs. Arthur Guiterman, for use of the couplet on the title page;

Harper & Brothers, for use of Bible passages on pages 55, 67, 83, and 101, as found in *The Holy Bible, A New Translation,* by James Moffatt, copyrighted in 1935 by Harper & Brothers.

First Printing May 1950
Second Printing October 1951
Third Printing May 1954
Fourth Printing November 1957
Fifth Printing April 1963
Sixth Printing July 1963

COPYRIGHT, 1950, BY FRIENDSHIP PRESS, INC.
Printed in the United States of America

DESIGNED BY LOUISE E. JEFFERSON

CONTENTS

FOREWORD
[7]

Section One
WAKE UP AND SING
[9]

Section Two
SINGING AT WORK AND PLAY
[19]

Section Three
FRIENDS IN MANY PLACES
[39]

Section Four
IN OUR HOMES
[55]

Section Five
WATCH AND WONDER
[67]

Section Six
DAYS OF JOY
[83]

Section Seven
TOGETHER IN WORSHIP
[101]

FOREWORD

For a long time I have wanted to harvest a sheaf of songs from fields near and far and bind them together between the covers of one beautiful book. This would be full of the common fare of joy and play, of work and worship that sustains all children in every country. If such a book can be produced and widely distributed, I believe that the understanding and unity so wistfully desired at present can be strengthened through singing together the most vivid songs conceived by a great variety of peoples.

Since we are all "bound together in the bundle of life with God," wherever or whenever we break into song we celebrate the very stuff of existence by which each and every group live. Richard Cabot in *What Men Live By* says these essentials are work, play, love, and worship. These are surely what all human beings sing about at home, in church, and when they long for companionship or relax in recreation.

"The Realm of God" is within us—every one of us—and the entire round of our daily living lies within that province. Turning the commonplace into music is a universal art, not the possession of any sect or locality, and the very essence of religion is the singing heart that expresses itself in a marvelous variety of ways. When we come to this realization, possessed so fully by Jesus, when we sing together what any and all of us have experienced of our divine kinship, we are "brothers under the skin." Music somehow has the power to help us feel ourselves tied together with "the golden cord, close binding *all* mankind" through the spirit of him who practiced the oneness of the children of God. The voice of every people must be heard to give this dynamic truth full meaning, and the lifting of all voices in chorus attests its reality.

The songs that make up this book were chosen to touch off sparks of wonder, friendliness, laughter, and appreciation, as they kindle love of the Unseen. The worship section particulary seeks to chart the curve of a growing child's religion—"first the blade, then the ear, then the full grain in the ear."

The song sources will stamp the origin of the grain garnered. More significant will be the uses to which the songs are appropriated, as a feast that is shared when we break bread together as a company.

Our aims are tremendously important, now that we know we must have "one world" or none. How to train children to govern their emotions and their wills in order to fit them to become citizens of one world depends in large measure upon the degree to which we help them to become Christians. In this process music and poetry, inspired by the truly religious spirit, wield a large influence.

The concept of regard for the individual as a being of particular worth to God and of children as precious in his sight can be effectively transmitted through musical means. The use of music for this end demands study, skill, and consecration. We are inspired by the Eternal's word to Job: ". . . the morning stars sang together and the sons of God shouted for joy." We have faith that the spiritual laws that uphold the universe are supporting all those who work for the accomplishment of such high purposes.   E.L.T.

New York City
June, 1950

:1:

WAKE UP AND SING

*I opened the doors of my heart,
And behold,
There was music within
And a song!*

—Jean Ingelow

SECTION ONE
SUGGESTIONS FOR SINGING

Let All the World, page 12. As this is an antiphon, or responsive song, let the chorus sing, "Let all the world in every corner sing: My God and King!" Then one voice or a small group of voices may respond to the call, using the other lines.

Come Out to Play, page 13. The jolly English round suggests any number of rhythmic actions—clapping, skipping, dancing. The round may be sung in unison until the melody is learned. Then three groups may be formed with a strong leader to steer each one. Group I starts doing the first line alone and continues singing the three lines through three times. When Group I reaches the second line, Group II begins the first and also does the whole round three times over. When Group II reaches the second line, Group III pipes up and keeps going on three times, also without stopping. This kind of singing is an easy way to sing in harmony.

FELLOWSHIP OF SONG

Arthur Guiterman

Adapted from Handel's
"Harmonious Blacksmith"

Flowing

When your voice with eve - ry o - ther's Joins to lift the tune a - long, All are com - rades, friends and bro - thers In the fel - low - ship of song.

Since music is the language that belongs to everybody, we find new friends through singing together. Thus we can enlarge our fellowship to include all nations, races, and religions. In this number we are united in a singing comradeship by means of a tune composed in England over two hundred years ago and the verse of a modern American poet.

Words used by permission of Mrs. Arthur Guiterman.

LET ALL THE WORLD

All the World

George Herbert, 1593-1633

John Porter, 1877-

Briskly

1. Let all the world in eve-ry cor-ner sing: My God and King! The heavens are not too high, His praise may thi-ther fly; The earth is not too low, His prai-ses there may grow. Let all the world in eve-ry cor-ner sing: My God and King!

2. Let all the world in eve-ry cor-ner sing: My God and King! The Church with psalms must shout, No door can keep them out: But, more than all, the heart Must bear the lon-gest part. Let all the world in eve-ry cor-ner sing: My God and King!

Music copyright, 1934, by Robert G. McCutchan.
Used by permission.

DOING NOTHING BUT SING

Old English Rhyme
Alsatian Folk Song

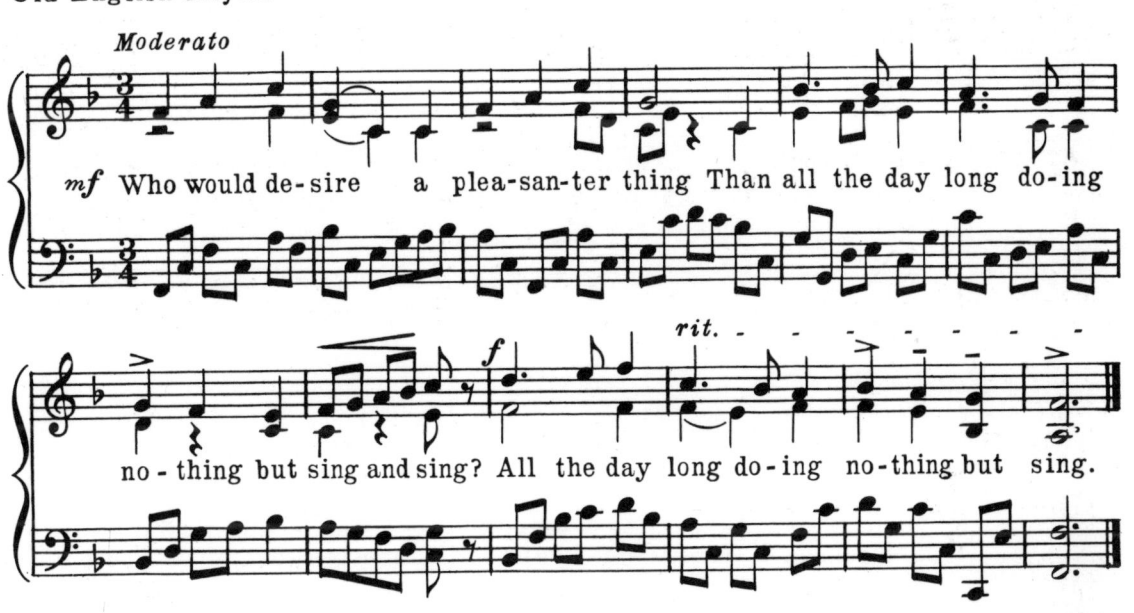

Moderato

mf Who would de-sire a plea-san-ter thing Than all the day long do-ing no-thing but sing and sing? All the day long do-ing no-thing but sing.

COME OUT TO PLAY

Old Rhyme
English Tune

Gaily

1. Girls and boys, come out to play! We must have a ho-li-day. Heigh-o! Heigh-o! Have a ho-li-day.
2. If you want hay sweet and fine Rake it when the sun doth shine. Heigh-o! Heigh-o! When the sun doth shine.

From *Vermont Folk Songs and Ballads*. Used by permission of Arthur Wallace Peach, agent for the Vermont Commission on Country Life, 6 Prospect Street, Northfield, Vermont.

CANTICLE TO THE SUN

St. Francis, 1225
Translated by Sophie Jewett

Adapted from
Giovanni Guidetti, 16th C.

Moderato

1. O Lord, we praise thee for our Bro-ther Sun, Who brings us day, who brings us gol-den light; He tells us of thy beau-ty, Ho-ly One. We praise thee, too, when falls the qui-et night, For Si-ster Moon and eve-ry sil-ver
2. For our brave Bro-ther Wind we give thee praise; For clouds and stor-my skies, for gen-tle air; And for our Si-ster Wa-ter, cool and fair, Who does us ser-vice in sweet hum-ble ways; But when the win-ter dar-kens bit-ter
3. For our good friend, so mer-ry and so bold, Dear Bro-ther Fire, beau-ti-ful and strong; For our good Mo-ther Earth, we praise thee, Lord; For the bright flowers she scat-ters eve-ry-where, For all the fruit and grain her fields af-

[14]

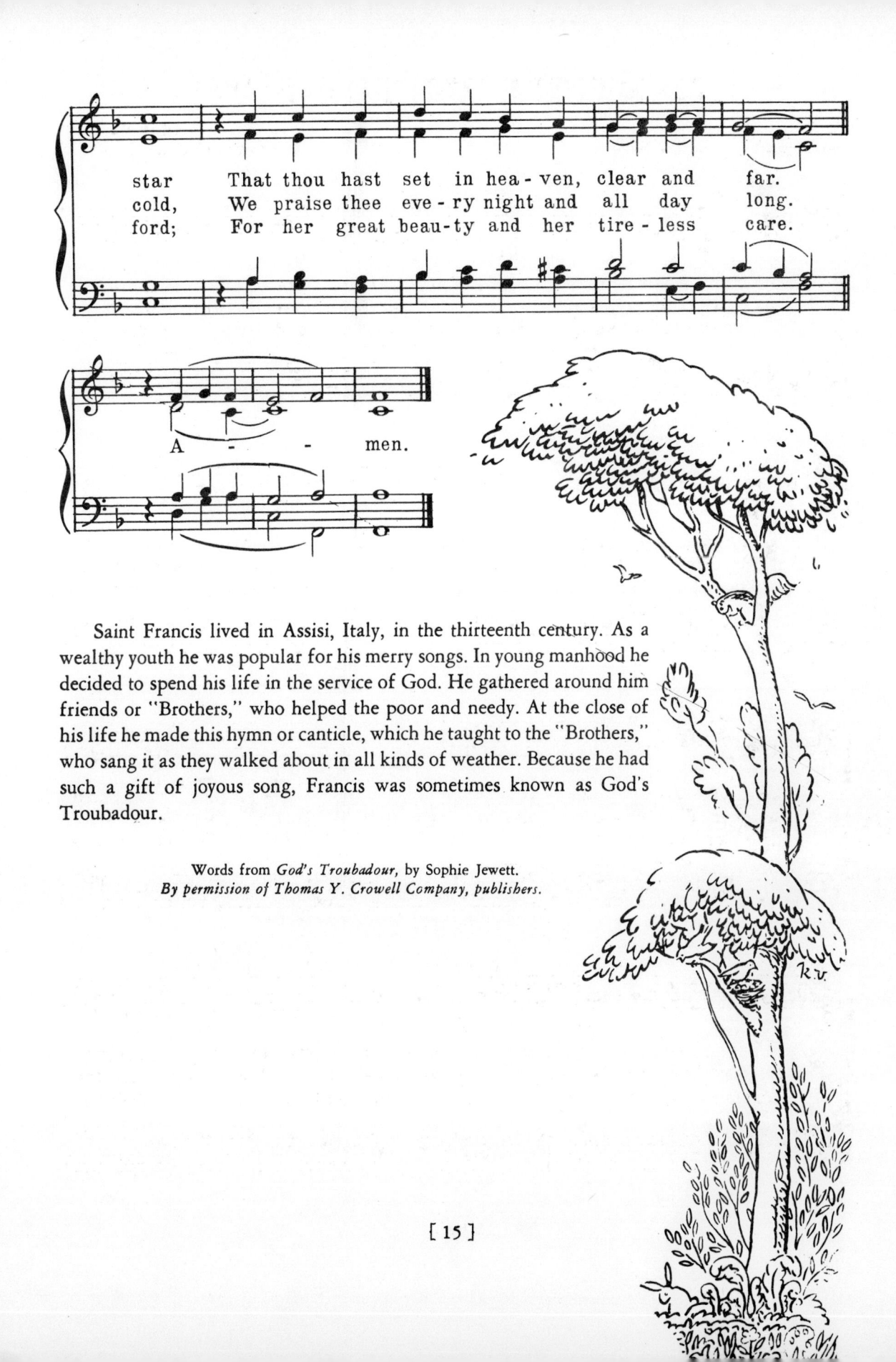

star	That thou hast set in hea-ven, clear and far.
cold,	We praise thee eve-ry night and all day long.
ford;	For her great beau-ty and her tire-less care.

A - - men.

Saint Francis lived in Assisi, Italy, in the thirteenth century. As a wealthy youth he was popular for his merry songs. In young manhood he decided to spend his life in the service of God. He gathered around him friends or "Brothers," who helped the poor and needy. At the close of his life he made this hymn or canticle, which he taught to the "Brothers," who sang it as they walked about in all kinds of weather. Because he had such a gift of joyous song, Francis was sometimes known as God's Troubadour.

Words from God's Troubadour, by Sophie Jewett.
By permission of Thomas Y. Crowell Company, publishers.

THE PIPER

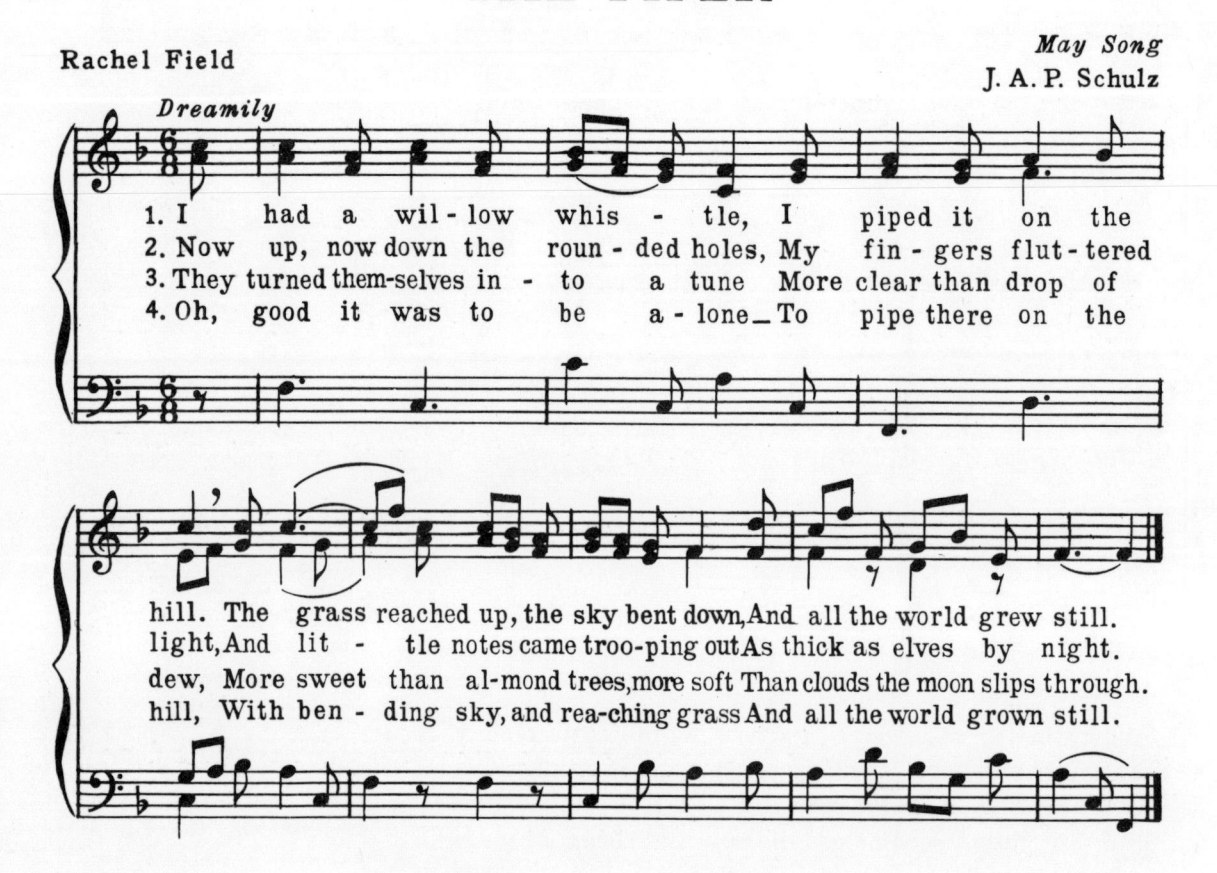

Rachel Field

May Song
J. A. P. Schulz

Dreamily

1. I had a wil-low whis-tle, I piped it on the hill. The grass reached up, the sky bent down, And all the world grew still.
2. Now up, now down the roun-ded holes, My fin-gers flut-tered light, And lit-tle notes came troo-ping out As thick as elves by night.
3. They turned them-selves in-to a tune More clear than drop of dew, More sweet than al-mond trees, more soft Than clouds the moon slips through.
4. Oh, good it was to be a-lone — To pipe there on the hill, With ben-ding sky, and rea-ching grass And all the world grown still.

From the very earliest times to the present day man has made instruments on which to play. Probably one of the first instruments was the wooden whistle, and it is still in common use today. In this song a child has made a whistle out of a willow stem and is playing a tune as he sits on a hilltop.

Words from *Pointed People*, by Rachel Field.
By permission of The Macmillan Company, publishers.

YOUTH

Langston Hughes
Composer Unknown

In marching measure

We have to-mor-row Bright be-fore us Like a flame.
Yes-ter-day A night-gone thing, A sun-down name. And
dawn to-day Broad arch a-bove the road we came. We march! We march!

In a Cleveland, Ohio, high school, Langston Hughes began making poetry. His poems are popular with young people because he knows how to put into words the thoughts and feelings of his own Negro people, and he understands the eagerness of all boys and girls to live life fully.

Words reprinted from *The Dream Keeper*, by Langston Hughes, *by permission of Alfred A Knopf, Inc.* Copyright, 1932, by Alfred A. Knopf, Inc.

THANKS TO GOD

From the Portuguese
by Antônio de Campos Gonçalves

Brazilian Folk Song

Flowing

1. In the morning when I waken, As I kneel and make my prayer, I give thanks to God, the Father, For his tender love and care.
2. When at night the stars are shining, Many children far and near, Talk with God and ask his blessing, Sleep in peace and know no fear.

The melody comes from the central section of the country and was the first folk tune to be used in the New Evangelical Hymn Book of Brazil.

Copyright, 1950, by Friendship Press.

:2:

SINGING AT WORK AND PLAY

Give us, oh, give us,

    the man who sings at his work...

He does more in the same time—

    he will do it better—

    he will persevere longer.

—Thomas Carlyle

SECTION TWO
SUGGESTIONS FOR SINGING

Planting Rice, page 22. To feel how hard the work really is, the children may bend over as if setting out plants in a straight row and try singing with the Filipino planter in time with the action. You may find it necessary to have some children sing while others plant.

Round of the Oats, page 23. To play this French singing game, the children may form a circle and choose a leader to stand in the center. The group imitates in perfect rhythm the leader as he makes the motions of sowing seed, bending knees slightly, pretending to sit down, stamping, clapping, moving around the land to right or left (as refrain is sung). As refrain ends, the leader beckons one from the circle to take his place as leader for the second stanza. This plan is followed until six leaders have taken turns or everyone in the ring has been in the center.

Before Dinner, page 26. The leader may sing the description of what is being done, while children dramatize the action of the story and sing the chorus in strongly accented rhythm. The children clap their hands to each "Ya, ya."

The Carpenter, page 27. The children may tap out as many different patterns of sounds as they can think of to imitate the music the tools make when the carpenter puts them to work.

Seeds We Bring, page 30. To enter into the life of these African Christians the children may act out this ceremony (see note below hymn).

Fruits and Vegetables, page 31. One child may play that he is a fruit and vegetable seller, carrying a basket of fruit and vegetables on his head, as he goes around the group inviting the others to buy.

Sung at Harvest Time, page 32. To picture these scenes, tableaux may be posed and the song sung with appropriate actions. Or a march of harvest hands may be arranged with accompanying drum, trumpet, and song. The workers may carry stalks of ripened corn, sickles, and baskets filled with gathered grain.

Ploughing, page 38. Imagine two farm workers whistling soprano and alto parts. First have the whole group whistle the soprano part, then the alto. Divide the group into soprano and alto sections and practice whistling together. Then the song may be sung.

WORKERS TOGETHER

John C. Irwin
Finnish Folk Song

Earnestly

1. O God, thy rain and sun and soil Are joined, with human toil, To bring, from every clime and land, These bounties to our hand.
2. We thank thee, God, for sun and soil, Our brother man for toil; Apart from all not one could live, And so our thanks we give.

The poem was written for a youth conference group in the United States to sing as a grace before eating together. The folk song music from Finland is joined to it to help one realize how dependent we are on one another for music as well as food.

Words by permission of the author.

PLANTING RICE

Adapted from Visayan and Tagalog
By Abbie Farwell Brown

Filipino Folk Song

Ploddingly

Plan-ting rice is ne-ver fun, Bent from morn 'til set of sun;

Can-not stand and can-not sit, Can-not rest for a lit-tle bit.

Plan-ting rice is no fun, Bent from morn 'til set of sun;

Can-not stand, can-not sit, Can-not rest for a lit-tle bit.

From *The Philippine Progressive Music Series*, Book One, copyright 1924, 1948, *by special permission of the authors and publishers, Silver Burdett Company, New York.*

ROUND OF THE OATS

From the French French Folk Song

With strong accent

1. Who wants to hear, who wants to know, Just how our oats we're so-wing?

My fa-ther al-ways sowed them so, Then sat him down to rest a-while.

He stamped his foot, he clapped his hands, And went the round of all his lands.

REFRAIN *(after each stanza)*

'Tis oats and fair good wea-ther That al-ways come to-ge-ther.

The story of the oats is continued by substituting for the words *sowing* in the first line and *sowed* in the second line as follows:

Verse 2 *reaping* and *reaped*
Verse 3 *binding* and *bound*
Verse 4 *piling* and *piled*
Verse 5 *threshing* and *threshed*
Verse 6 *winnow* and *winnowed*

From *Sixty Folk Songs of France*, published and copyrighted (1915) by Oliver Ditson Company. *Used by permission.*

A-FISHING

From J. D. Okae

Singing Game
Gold Coast, Africa
From J. D. Okae

Playfully

We come, we come! We come, we come! We are fi-sher-men. We come out a-fi-shing, Oh! We come out a-fi-shing, Oh! Haul the fish in, Catch them, so!

Yea-b'o, yea-b'o! Yea-b'o, yea-b'o! Ye-yea-fare-fo. Ye-baa mpa-taa-yi, Mon-hwe! Ye-baa mpa-taa-yi, Mon-hwe! Se-nea yek-yere won, Mon-hwe!

Used by permission of J. D. Okae.

EVERY SMALL INCH OF FARM LAND
(El Pericón)

Carlos Roxlo
From Uruguay
Arranged by G. Grasso

Allegro moderato

1. Eve-ry small inch of farm land brings forth its blade of wheat, Which springs from the earth mo-ther quite rea-dy and sweet.
2. This old dance was danced by peo-ple that we ne-ver can know; They sang it, and they played it in days long a-go.
3. In their tri-umphs and their hard-ships Ar-ti-gas and his men Sang this song round their camp-fires Let's sing it a-gain!

This is the national dance of Uruguay. General Artigas was a great leader who corresponds to George Washington in United States history.

From *Canciones Panamericanas*, copyright, 1942, *by special permission of the publishers, Silver Burdett Company, New York.*

BEFORE DINNER

Carol Hart Sayre

Congo Children's Song
Arranged by Carol Hart Sayre

Rhythmically

SOLO: First we go to hoe our gar-den, ALL: Ya, ya, ya, ya.

SOLO: Next we car-ry jugs of wa-ter, ALL: Ya, ya, ya, ya.

SOLO: Then we pound the yel-low corn, ALL: Ya, ya, ya, ya.

SOLO: Then we stir our pots of mush, ALL: Ya, ya, ya, ya.

SOLO: Now we eat — come, ga-ther round the camp-fire, ALL: Ya, ya, ya, ya.

This song from the Lunda tribe of the Belgian Congo describes the duties that the women and girls have in preparing a meal. One girl sings the story, and all the others join in the chorus: "Ya, ya, ya, ya."

Copyright, 1950, by Friendship Press.

THE CARPENTER

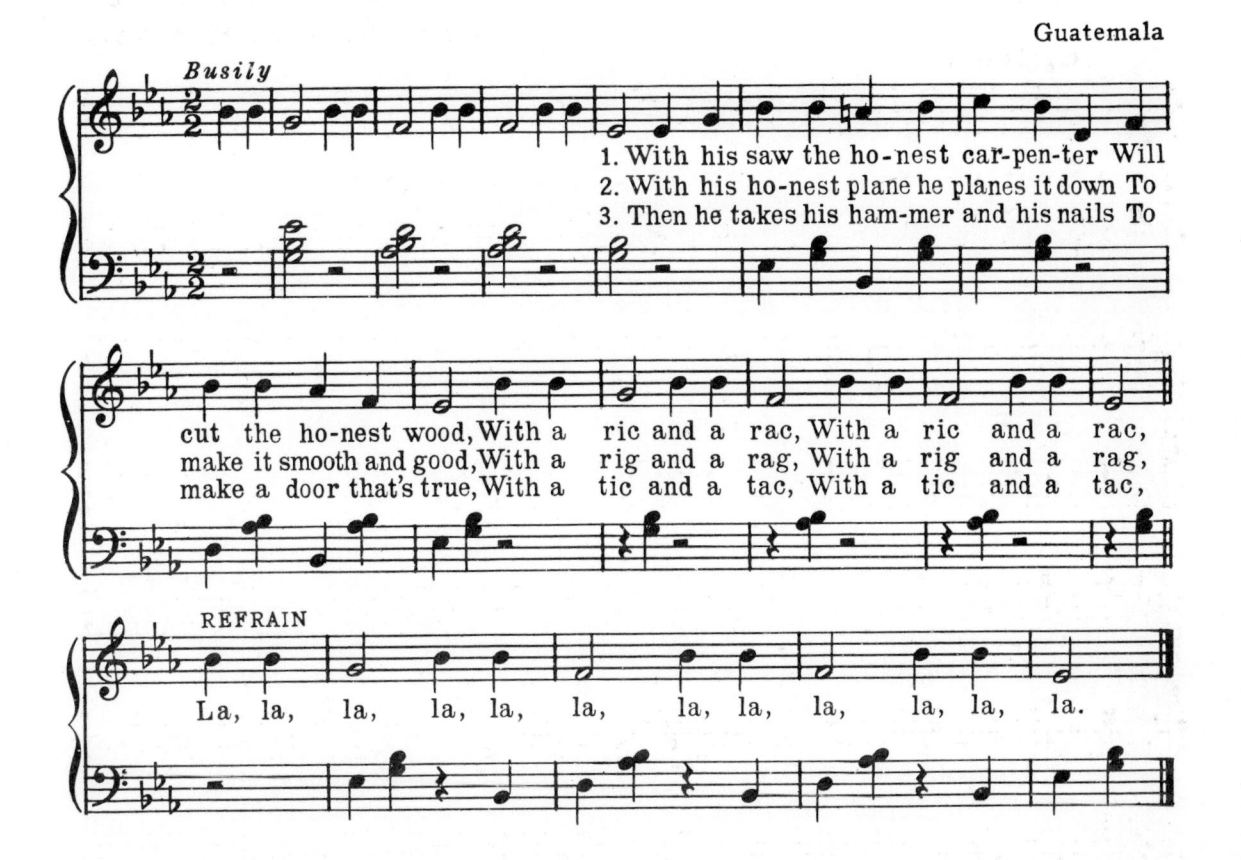

Guatemala

Busily

1. With his saw the ho-nest car-pen-ter Will cut the ho-nest wood, With a ric and a rac, With a ric and a rac,
2. With his ho-nest plane he planes it down To make it smooth and good, With a rig and a rag, With a rig and a rag,
3. Then he takes his ham-mer and his nails To make a door that's true, With a tic and a tac, With a tic and a tac,

REFRAIN

La, la, la, la, la, la, la, la, la, la, la, la.

4. He makes cabinets and chairs and things
   For homes for me and you,
   With a ric and a rac,
   With a ric and a rac, (REFRAIN)

5. With his saw and plane the carpenter
   Makes many things of wood,
   With a tic and a tac,
   With a tic and a tac, (REFRAIN)

The fisherman, the farmer, the seaman, and the carpenter are men we cannot get along without. This is the song of a jolly carpenter who sings as he works. You can almost tell what tool he is using by the sound of the words he sings—the saw goes "ric, rac," the hammer "tic, tac," etc.

From *Canciones Panamericanas*, copyright, 1942, by special permission of the publishers, Silver Burdett Company, New York.

MAKING MAPLE SUGAR

Based on Melody of a
Chippewa Medicine Man

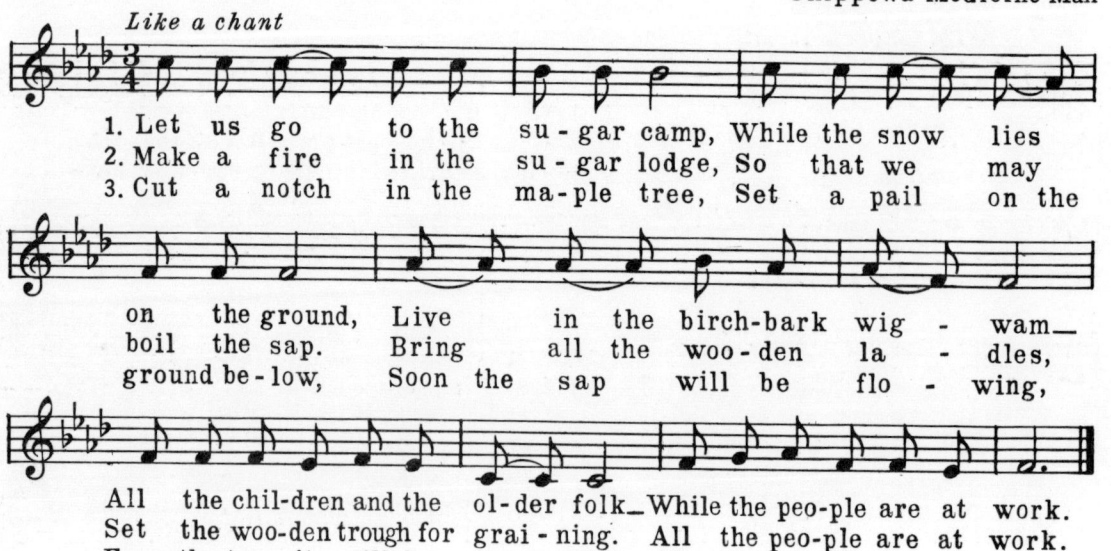

Like a chant

1. Let us go to the sugar camp, While the snow lies on the ground, Live in the birch-bark wigwam— All the children and the older folk— While the people are at work.
2. Make a fire in the sugar lodge, So that we may boil the sap. Bring all the wooden ladles, Set the wooden trough for graining. All the people are at work.
3. Cut a notch in the maple tree, Set a pail on the ground below, Soon the sap will be flowing, From the tree it will be flowing— All the people are at work.

4. In the snow see the rabbit tracks,
   Hear the note of the chickadee,
   We must not stop to follow them,
   'Tis the season of the sugar camp.
   All the people are at work.

5. Bring the sap from the maple trees,
   Pour the sap in the iron pot.
   See how it steams and bubbles.
   May we have a little taste of it?
   All the people are at work.

6. Pour the syrup in the graining trough,
   Stir it slowly as it thicker grows,
   Now it has changed to sugar,
   We may eat it in a birchbark dish,
   There is sugar for us all.

Early spring, in the lake-bordering forests of Minnesota and Wisconsin, is the time when Indians set up wigwams under the great trees. A Chippewa medicine man sang this song to help his people obtain a large supply of maple sugar.

Collected by Frances Densmore, Bureau of American Ethnology, Smithsonian Institution.
Paraphrased in English by Frances Densmore and *used by permission*.

YANGTZE BOATMEN'S CHANTEY

English by Bliss Wiant Chinese Chantey

With marked accent

Ri - ver boat-men, we, Toi - ling night and day.
Yah, hoo, Yah, hoo, hey! Yah, hoo, Yah, hoo, hey!

Backs ben-ding, Ropes tight'-ning, Sing we loud our lay.
Yai, yai, yai, Hai, yai, yai, Yah, hoo, Yah, hoo, hey!

This song is popular among the men who pull boats against the stream of the mighty Yangtze River. In rain or shine, heat or cold, the boatmen work to the rhythm of the chant. Such work songs as this formed almost the only kind of group vocal music in China before Christian missionaries taught the Chinese to sing hymns.

From *The Pagoda: Thirteen Chinese Songs*, compiled by Bliss Wiant, published by Cooperative Recreation Service, Delaware, Ohio.
Copyright, 1946, by Cooperative Recreation Service.

SEEDS WE BRING

The Reverend Julian S. Rea   Portuguese East Africa

Reverently, slowly chanting

LEADER
1. Seeds we bring, Lord, to thee,
2. Hoes we bring, Lord, to thee,
3. Hands we bring, Lord, to thee,
4. Ourselves we bring, Lord, to thee,

CHORUS
Wilt thou bless them, O Lord.
Wilt thou bless them, O Lord.
Wilt thou bless them, O Lord.
Wilt thou bless us, O Lord.

A song sung at Kambine, Portuguese East Africa. When the planting season begins, a little group of Christians carry their garden tools to the church and ask God's blessing upon them in song. The women and girls carry hoes and baskets of seeds and lay them on the altar, while the leader chants the first line of the music and the group sings the second line. The teacher talks about how the seeds must be planted in the right way and all the people must work hard to help the seeds grow. Hoes and seeds are left on the altar all night. At sunrise the people return and sing the last verse. Then, taking hoes and seeds, they go to their gardens singing, "The man who is happy is the one who digs," and so on, covering the following activities: plants, tends his crops, has a good harvest.

From *Child Guidance in Christian Living*. Copyright, 1945,
Stone and Pierce. *Used by permission.*

FRUITS AND VEGETABLES

From the Marathi of
Kashinath Jogdand
Translated by Clara L. Seiler

From India
Music Notation by
Emily R. Bissell

Recitative style (girl comes singing, basket on head)

REFRAIN: Buy vege-ta-bles! Po-ta-toes for you! you! I've spi-nach and greens! I've spi-nach and greens! I've spi-nach and greens! I've spi-nach and greens!

1. On-ions, egg-plant, gar-lic and ca-ra-way! Greens of ca-ra-way! Yea!
2. Pine-ap-ples, po-me-los, sweet limes and o-ran-ges! Pome-gra-nates, too! Who?
3. Bull's-hearts, cus-tard ap-ples, please come, and taste my gua-vas! Fruit, vege-ta-bles, come, buy! Aye!

Used by permission of Emily R. Bissell.

SUNG AT HARVEST TIME

Peruvian

Espressivo (♩ = 72)

Come, my sisters, come, my brothers, At the sounding of the horn; On the hill-sides, on the mountains, Har-vest we the yel-low corn. Gol-den shines our Fa-ther Sun;

[32]

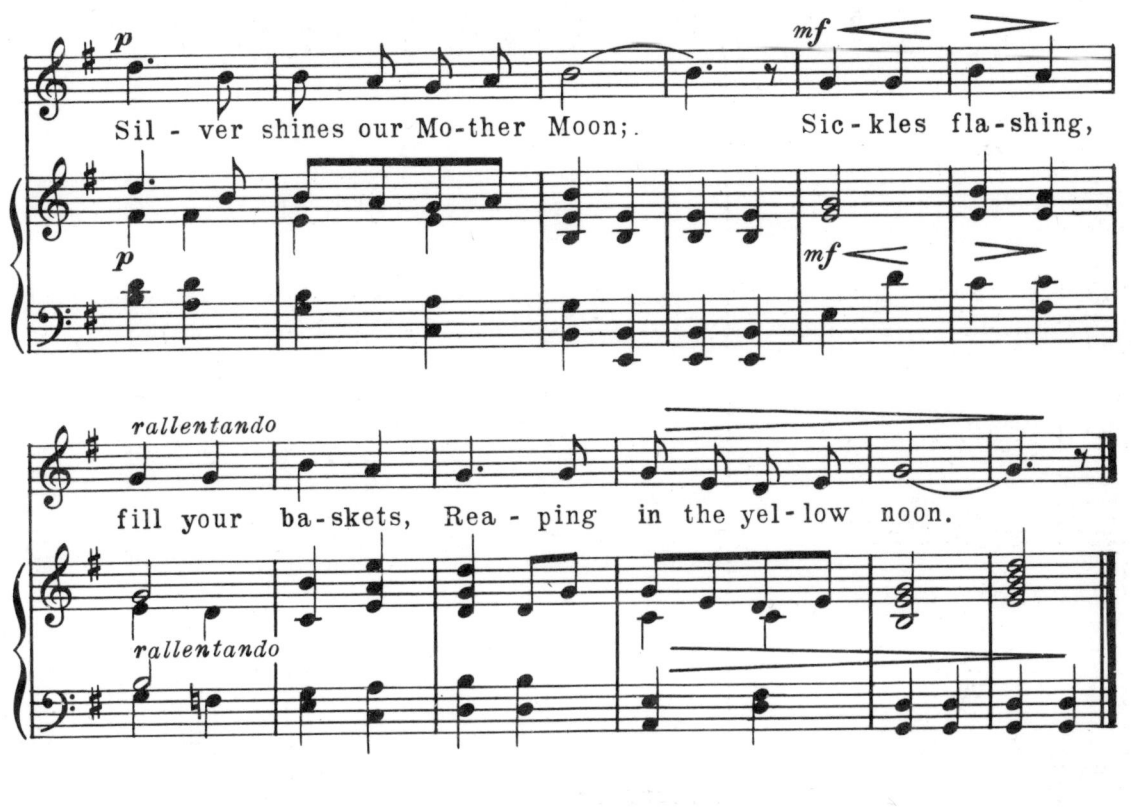

Sil - ver shines our Mo-ther Moon;. Sic-kles fla-shing,

rallentando

fill your ba-skets, Rea-ping in the yel-low noon.

When the grain is ripe in the fields of Peru, there is rejoicing because a new store of food is ready. The gathering party is a time for song and dance. In our song the words and music suggest tableaux or actions that picture the harvest scene.

From *The Latin-American Song Book*, copyright, 1942. *Used by permission of Ginn and Company, owners of the copyright.*

SHAWL WEAVER'S SONG

Seymour Barnard   Cashmere Folk Song

Allegretto

Def-tly, def-tly, nim-ble fin-gers, Weave gold and a-zure strands.

Hast-en, hast-en, he who lin-gers, Fly, firm and fa-cile hands.

Weave for mo-ther's shoul-der Shawls gay with glint of gold;

For her when bent and ol-der, Warm wool a-gainst the cold.

The softest wool grows under the coat of the goat found in Kashmir (sometimes spelled "Cashmere") in the mountain region of northern India. Light, warm shawls are woven from it, in intricate designs of rich color. How dreamy is the song the weaver sings, working long hours at the loom, weaving, weaving the beautiful cloth that will help keep some mother comfortable.

WITH NEEDLE AND THREAD

Flower Ula
Folk Song from Hawaii and American Samoa

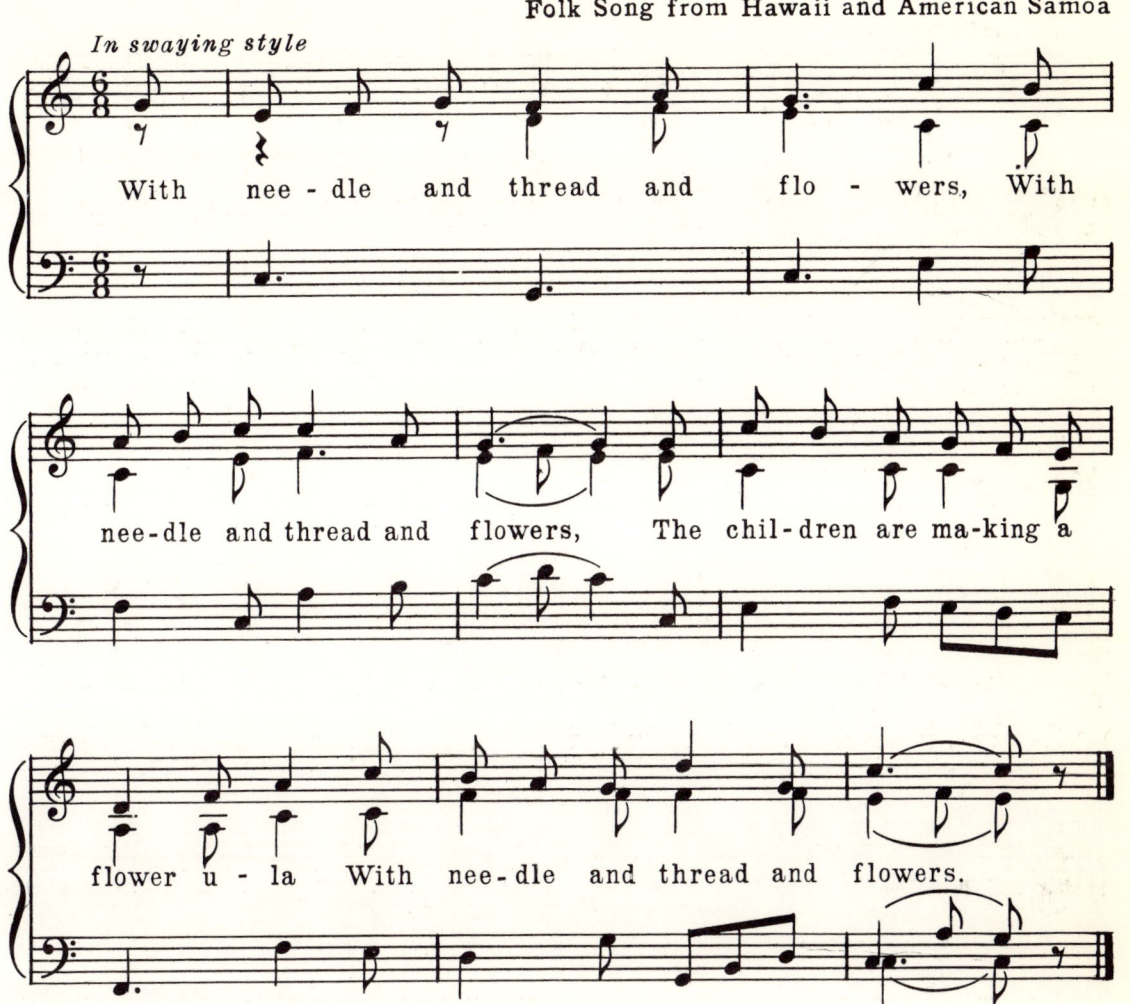

In swaying style

With nee-dle and thread and flo - wers, With nee-dle and thread and flowers, The chil-dren are ma-king a flower u - la With nee-dle and thread and flowers.

The grade school children in Hawaii and in Tutuila, American Samoa, sing when a big steamship from the United States brings tourists to their island home. Flower chains, called *ulas,* are made by stringing blossoms of many hues together. The flower chains are hung about the necks of the visitors. This song is used to greet the guests as they land.

Transcribed by Mrs. W. A. Coulter at Tutuila School. Collected by Charles Hofmann and *used by his permission.*

CALLING THE COWS

Tyrolese Yodel

Don't hurry

f Hark to the cow-herd's mer-ry cal-ling, mer-ri-ly Oh! mer-ri-ly Oh! Hark to the e-choes soft-ly fal-ling, mer-ri-ly Oh! mer-ri-ly Oh! Through the mor-ning air when the day is fair, Through the mor-ning air when the

[36]

day is fair, Echoing 'mid the hills and valleys, merrily Oh! merrily Oh! Merrily, merrily, merrily Oh! Merrily Oh! merrily Oh! *(Repeat like an echo)*

(Repeat pp)

The Tyrol is a part of the mountainous Alpine country of Central Europe and a great place for dairying. The people who live in that district have a way of singing called "yodeling," their lower notes in a manlike and their upper notes in a woman-like voice. The folk music of these people is all "up and down," like the mountains among which they live.

From *The Dominion Song Book*, compiled by E. Douglas Tayler, Whitcombe & Tombs, Limited, New Zealand.

PLOUGHING

Balzamina
Czech Folk Song

Sweetly

1. Where will you go, My Johnnie, dear? I go to plough by waters clear.
2. I ploughed and ploughed; 'Twas all in vain— Over my field flood waters came.

f REFRAIN *(joyfully)*

Tra-la-la-la-la-la, Tra-la-la-la-la-la, la-la-la, Tra-la-la-la-la-la, Tra-la-la-la-la-la, Tra-la-la.

Farmers have to put up with many hindrances in raising their crops. They often surprise us with the cheerful way they keep on working, no matter what happens. In this song, imagine a Czech mother and son whistling two parts, the soprano and the alto lines.

Contributed by Robert Mokrejs.

: 3 :
FRIENDS IN MANY PLACES

Friends,
with no more sounds of discord,
Let us sing our hopeful songs.
Surely, as the stars above us,
Music to us all belongs!

—From "Ode to Joy," by Schiller

SECTION THREE
SUGGESTIONS FOR SINGING

From Every Land, page 42. Fill a tray with good things to eat and drink, choosing articles from different countries. See if the children can name the lands from which they come and how they were brought to the home table. More surprising might be the discovery of the men and women whose songs are in this book. If their homelands were visited, it would take much travel to reach all these countries around the globe. How many languages would have to be learned before any conversation could begin!

Friendship Song, page 45. "How large is your friendship circle?" Put the question to the children and list on a blackboard or paper the people they know, write to, or read about, who live in different countries or who belong to different races or religions. Name one child to represent each until all names have been called. Make a circle of representatives to see how big or small is its size. Another time stick pins on a map of the world to locate the homes of all these friends.

Hail, Guest, page 46. The open-hearted, friendly attitude of this stanza breathes a welcoming spirit that everyone needs to cultivate in the world of today. Arthur Guiterman's lines might stimulate the children to write another stanza. Of several possibilities that may occur to them one might be the guest's acceptance, describing what he'd like to find in the home of his host. Another addition could continue the invitation by telling what the host has in his home that he would like to share with the guest. Experiment with extra verses and take down what the boys and girls suggest as they express their understanding of the grace of hospitality.

The Magic Tom-Tom, page 51. To suggest the sound made by the tom-tom have the children cup the palms of both hands, lay thumbs tightly against pointer fingers, press fingers together, and fit sides of thumbs and tips of fingers so that each one matches its mate. In order to produce a deep, muffled tone-beat, as the children clap the rhythm have them keep palms hollow and fingers close together so that there are no spaces between them. The tom-tom may be played all the way through on the first and third beats of each measure or on every "boom," "magic tom-tom," "magic beat," and "Oh, dance and sing!", the beats being marked by whatever ways are suggested by the group. Finally, have the children follow the pattern of beating that is voted to be the most realistic treatment of the song story.

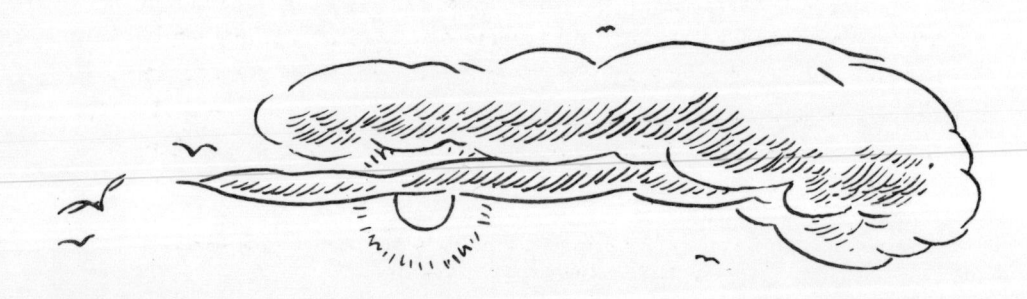

OUR BEAUTIFUL EARTH

Frances E. Jacobs   German Folk Song

Allegretto espressivo

mf How beautiful is the green earth, The stars in the heaven above! But what would the whole world be worth If we did not fill it with Love, with Love, If we did not fill it with Love?

Frances E. Jacobs asks a question in this song that any child should be able to answer. Long ago Paul taught persons newly become Christian that "... faith, hope, and love endure. These are the great three, and the greatest of them is love." (*I Corinthians* 13:13. *The Bible, An American Translation,* Smith and Goodspeed, the University of Chicago Press.)

From *Old Tunes with New Rhymes,* by Frances E. Jacobs, published and copyrighted (1931) by Oliver Ditson Company.

FROM EVERY LAND

Harry Webb Farrington　　　　　　　　From Queen Elizabeth's *Virginal Book*

Lightly

1. The world came to my home to-day To spread a won-drous feast; The ships and planes in bright ar-ray Brought gifts from West and East; From
2. The world came to my school to-day And brought me jol-ly games; The play-mates strange had naught to say, Nor told their stran-ger names; But
3. The world came to my church to-day, Their praise and gifts to bring; In eve-ry tongue to sing and pray And wor-ship Je-sus King. Not

[42]

> In - dia, spice; from Chi - na, tea, My
> all could laugh and play like me, Soft,
> as the Wise Men, ri - ding far To
>
> ta - ble high to fill; Each na - tion sent in
> warm were heart and hand, That made a ring strong
> find him in one place; His spi - rit, co - ming
>
> peace to me A to - ken of good will.
> as could be Of friends from eve - ry land.
> where we are, Binds hearts of eve - ry race.

Harry Webb Farrington was a minister who spent much time speaking and writing to American public school students to prepare them for world citizenship. Through his poem we are helped to visualize what ships, planes, and other modern inventions have done to bring all peoples close together. Not only food, but fun, friendliness, and worship are shared, and all of them help to bind us together in true fellowship.

Words used by permission of Mrs. Harry Webb Farrington.

ROUND THE WORLD

Jessie Eleanor Moore

Abendruh
Ferdinand Schultz

Thoughtfully

1. Our thoughts go round the world, To children eve-ry-where; So much of joy is ours, O God, Help us to love and share.
2. This world, our home, is big, But not too big to be A place where friend-li-ness, dear God, Makes us one fa-mi-ly.

Abendruh is the German word for "evening rest." Before sleeping it is good to travel on wings of song, thinking joy and love to other children far away.

Words from *Bible Stories for Children*. Copyright, The Pilgrim Press. *Used by permission.*

FRIENDSHIP SONG

Author Unknown
Words Altered

Composer Unknown

In marching rhythm

1. All children who live in distant lands With joyful song we greet! Hold out to us your friendly hands Our circle to complete. In countries far and countries near One family are we. The voice of friendship now we hear 'Cross continent and sea.

2. Then, boys and girls, as in our play Around the world we go, With mind and heart we'll try to-day Each other's lands to know. And when our time for playing flies, And when our childhood ends, May we, grown older and more wise, Be firm and loyal friends.

From *Creating a World of Friendly Children*, published by the Committee on World Friendship among Children, New York, 1932.

HAIL, GUEST

Door Verse
Arthur Guiterman

Welsh Carol

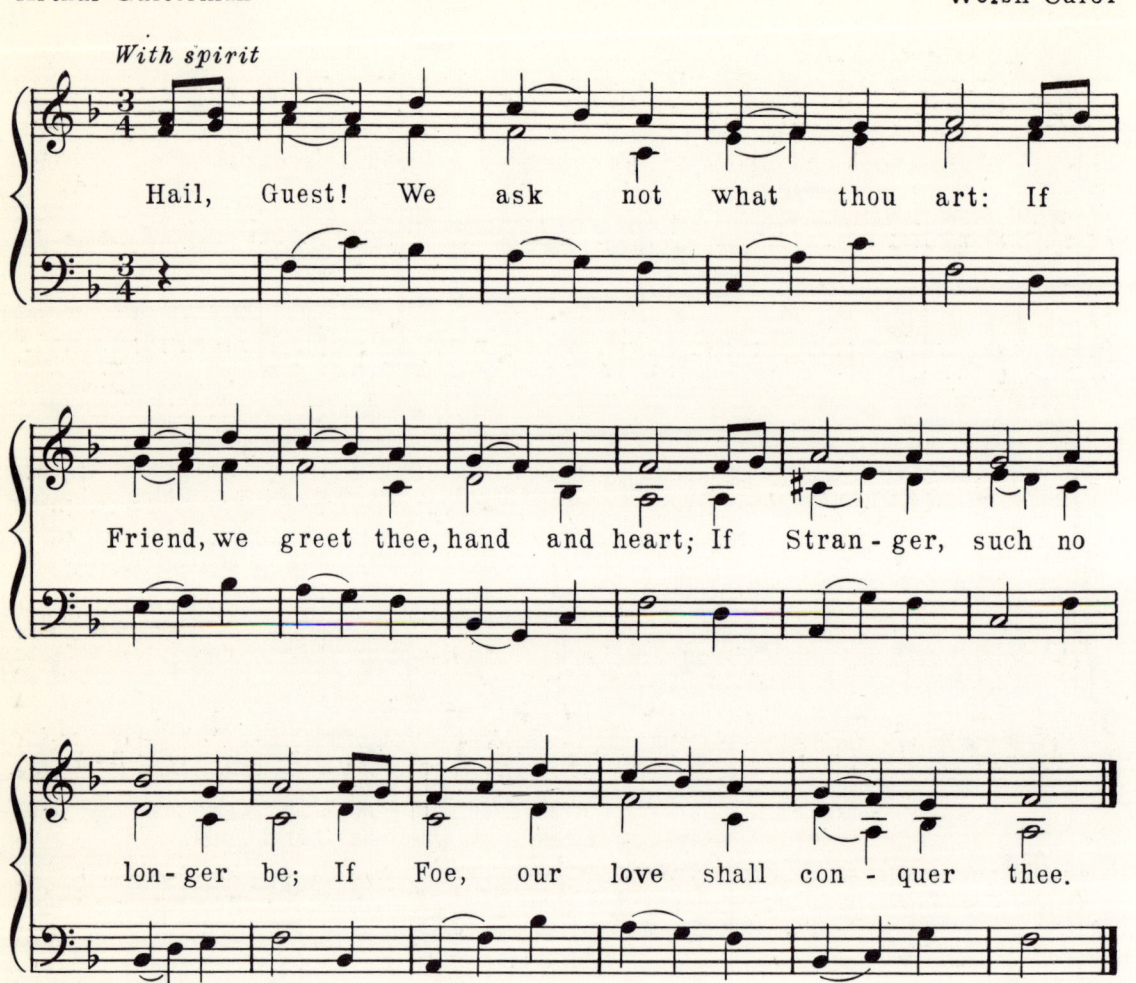

With spirit

Hail, Guest! We ask not what thou art: If Friend, we greet thee, hand and heart; If Stranger, such no longer be; If Foe, our love shall conquer thee.

It is a sign that a person is a Christian when he carries out the words of Jesus: ". . . I was a stranger and you welcomed me, . . . as you did it to one of the least of these my brethren, you did it to me." (*Matthew* 25: 35, 40. Revised Standard Version.)

Words taken from *Death and General Putnam and 101 Other Poems,* by Arthur Guiterman. Published and copyright, 1935, by E. P. Dutton & Co., Inc., New York.

CHUMS

Arthur Guiterman English Folk Song

Conversationally

1. You see, we three, Fred, Joe, and me Is chums. When I, "Hul-lo!" To Fred and Joe, They comes. 'Most eve-ry day We go and play some-wheres. If I've a bun, And they has none, We shares.

2. We all can slide; And Fred can ride, And swim, And make a kite! I think a sight Of him, And Jo-ey, too; He helps us do our sums, Be-cause, you see, Joe, Fred, and me Is chums.

The American poet, Arthur Guiterman, seems to be chuckling as he overhears a boy talking about his friends. Can you imagine one of the chums whistling the catchy English air, calling his friends out to play?

Words used by permission of Mrs. Arthur Guiterman.

TRAMPING

Based on the Hebrew Translation
of Sh. L. Gordon

Lag B'omer
Ch. Korchevsky

March time

We're off to the fo-rest, with friends a-tramp-ing we go, Where stret-ches of green are be-gin-ning now to show. The twit-ter of bird-songs an-noun-ces the dawn of day; We'll shrill with the lo-custs and fro-lic and play.

A holiday in the woods is one looked forward to by Jewish children. The bugle tones in the first and third melody lines suggest the children's anticipation of a day in the open.

Adapted from *Songs of Zion,* compiled and edited by Harry Coopersmith, Behrman House, Inc., Publishers, New York.

A RUSSIAN LANDSCAPE

E. Douglas Tayler · Russian Melody

Quick, strongly marked

1. Through the fo-rest blows the tem-pest, Loud the wind is wai - ling, Fro-zen lies the long, grey ri - ver, Red the sun - light fai - ling.
2. On the plain the snow lies dee-ply All the road-way li - ning, Night comes cree-ping o'er the land-scape, Hun - gry wolves are whi - ning.
3. Hark! the hoof-beats! Hark! the sleighbells! Safe - ly out of dan - ger Comes a trave-ler to the vil - lage, Wel - come to the stran - ger!

Russian music is strong, steady, and often sad. Long northern winters are apt to give the country a dreary look. The poem draws a picture of a cold, dangerous sleigh ride through the forest. What a relief when the traveler is welcomed out of the darkness to safety and warmth by friendly villagers!

From *The Dominion Song Book*, compiled by E. Douglas Tayler, Whitcombe & Tombs, Limited, New Zealand.

CANOE SONG

Arranged by E. Douglas Tayler

Poi Waka
Maori Song
New Zealand

Gently flowing, not too slowly

Now up and now down glides our ca-noe on-ward to Wai-a-ri-ki, See, see how the waves part from her prow, Sing i to ma-u-na-wa.

The ending *i to maunawa* is a refrain something like the old English *fa, la, la*, which makes a pleasing rhythm. It is pronounced *ee toh mah-oo-nah-wah.*

From *The Dominion Song Book*, compiled by E. Douglas Tayler, Whitcombe & Tombs, Limited, New Zealand.

THE MAGIC TOM-TOM

Carol Hart Sayre

From the Congo
Arranged by Carol Hart Sayre

Strongly accented, steady rhythm

Boom, boom, boom, boom, boom. Boom, boom, boom, boom, boom. Oh, listen to my magic tom-tom, Listen to its magic beat! All the birds hover near to chirp and sing, All the monkeys swing down with dancing feet. Oh, dance and sing! Oh, dance and sing!

The Lunda tribe of the Belgian Congo enjoy a story about a drum that was supposed to be magic because it could answer questions. Really there was a boy inside the drum. The storyteller stops at appropriate places in the story, and this chorus is sung by the listeners.

Copyright, 1950, by Friendship Press.

WHAT IS PEACE

Arranged by a Committee
from the Ideas of Children

Edith Lovell Thomas

    1. READING (leader)
        Peace is comfort
           That can be shared
              With others.

    REFRAIN (group)

Slowly, sustained

Peace is God's bles-sing u - pon the world.

    2. READING (leader)
        Peace is love,—
           The feeling of friendship,
              The happiness of everybody.

    REFRAIN (group)

    3. READING (leader)
        Peace is a thing
           That brings to all nations
              Something greater than gold.

    REFRAIN (group)

    4. READING (leader)
        Peace is joy
           Happiness
              Rest and love.

    REFRAIN (hummed by group)

*Words used by permission of the National Council for Prevention of War,
Washington, D. C.*

STUDY WAR NO MORE

Negro Spiritual

Allegro moderato

Goin' to lay down my sword and shield Down by the ri-ver-side, Down by the ri-ver-side, Down by the ri-ver-side. Goin' to lay down my sword and shield Down by the ri-ver-side, Ain't goin' stu-dy war no more. Ain't goin' stu-dy war no more, Ain't goin' stu-dy war no more, Ain't goin' stu-dy war no more, Ain't goin' stu-dy war no more.

Many times Negro spirituals interpret thoughts found in the Bible in a way to kindle the imagination. This song was inspired by Micah, an Old Testament prophet, who wrote long ago: "... they shall beat their swords into plowshares, and their spears into pruninghooks: nation shall not lift up a sword against nation, neither shall they learn war any more." (*Micah* 4:3, King James Version.)

OATH OF FRIENDSHIP

From the Chinese
By Arthur Waley

Chinese Folk Melody

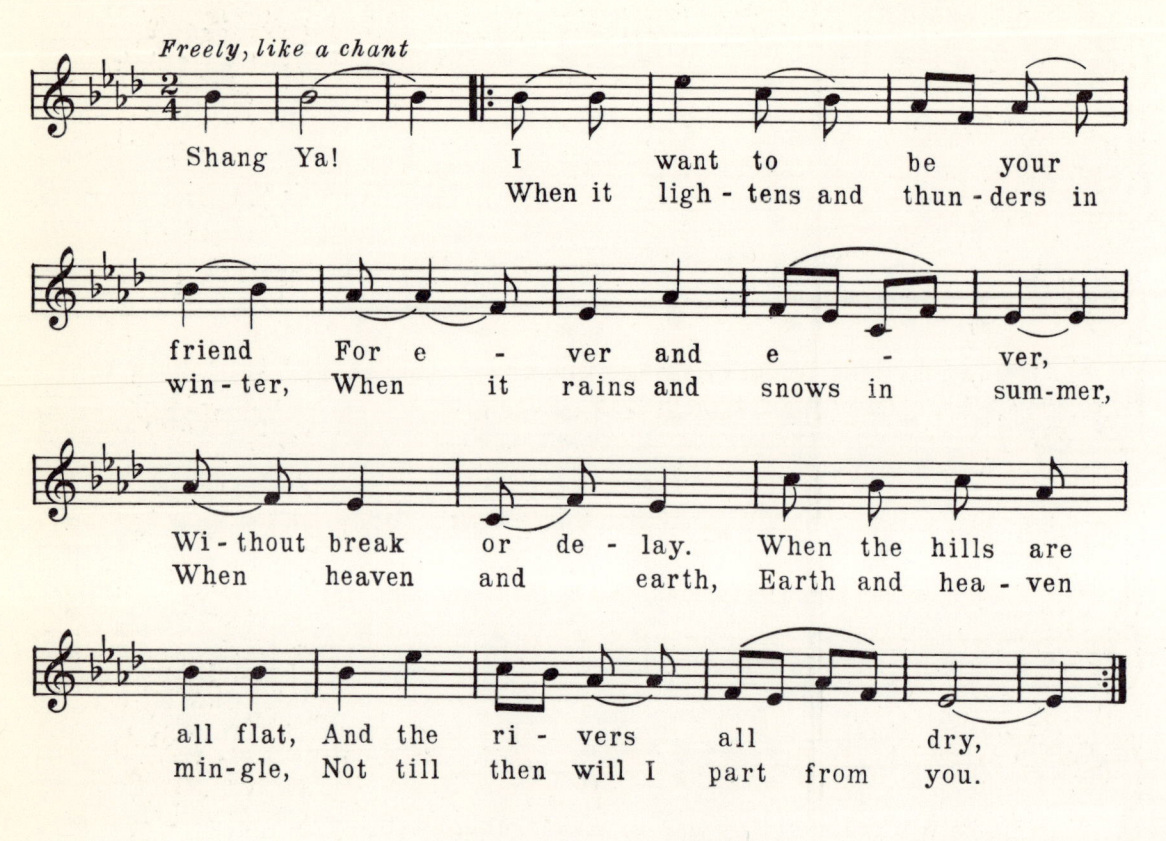

Freely, like a chant

Shang Ya! I want to be your friend For e-ver and e-ver, Wi-thout break or de-lay. When the hills are all flat, And the ri-vers all dry,

When itligh-tens and thun-ders in win-ter, When it rains and snows in sum-mer, When heaven and earth, Earth and hea-ven min-gle, Not till then will I part from you.

In southern China two men wanting to become friends build an altar of earth, and standing by it repeat this promise together. Chinese people have such a high regard for friends that they remain loyal to them whatever the cost.

Words from *170 Chinese Poems*, by Arthur Waley. *By permission of the publishers,*
Constable and Company, Ltd., London.
Melody contributed by Liu Liang-mo
to Charles Hofmann collection and *used with their permission.*

:4:

IN OUR HOMES

*The earth belongs to the Eternal...,
the world and its inhabitants.*

—Psalms 24: 1

SECTION FOUR
SUGGESTIONS FOR SINGING

Chinese Lullaby, page 60. The Chinese, in common with several other peoples, use in their music a five-tone scale instead of the seven-tone Western one we know. This tune may be played easily on the piano or organ by touching only black keys. Each tone is raised by playing it a half-step higher—that is, on the black key next above the note as written. Beginning on A sharp, only that key is needed with two blacks above—C sharp and D sharp—and two below—F sharp and G sharp. Try the same trick with the Japanese song "My Doll," on page 64, starting with F sharp.

Congo Lullaby, page 63. In the African Congo one hears the same five-tone scale that the Chinese and other folk like to sing. The mother sings only three of the five tones in her quieting lullaby. To find them on the piano, lower each tone as written a half-step to the black key next below it. Take G flat, then A flat next above it, and E flat next below it, and follow carefully the ups and downs and repeating of notes.

My Doll, page 64. See note above on "Chinese Lullaby."

GOD'S WORLD

Nancy Byrd Turner · · · Polish Folk Song

Smoothly

1. All the world is God's world; So we kneel and pray,
2. "When our sun is shi-ning, And our land is bright,
3. "When our day is o-ver, And our twi-light comes,

"Bless the o-ther chil-dren Far and far a-way!"
Their land's in the sha-dow, Keep them through the night!"
They are see-ing sun-rise, Bless them in their homes!"

4. Long the miles between us!
   Though we cannot call
   Over seas and mountains,
   God will bless us all!

Words used by permission of Nancy Byrd Turner.

[57]

A PRAYER OF THANKS

John Haynes Holmes
Alsatian Song

May be sung in unison or in two parts

1. O Father, thou who givest all The bounty of thy perfect love, We thank thee that upon us fall Such tender blessings from above.
2. We thank thee for the grace of home, For mother's love and father's care; For friends and teachers— all who come Our joys and hopes and fears to share.
3. For eyes to see and ears to hear, For hands to serve and arms to lift, For shoulders broad and strong to bear, For feet to run on errands swift.

    4. For faith to conquer doubt and fear,
        For love to answer every call,
        For strength to do, and will to dare,
        We thank thee, O thou Lord of all.

Words used by permission of the author.

SAMOA

American Samoa

Brightly

1. Rain-bows in the sky, Flo-wers eve-ry-where,
2. Sho-wers in the night, Per-fume all the day,

Gai-ly co-lored blos-soms, Love-ly isles so fair!
Where is there a coun-try Like Sa-mo-a Pe-le?

In the middle of the Pacific Ocean lie the tropical Samoan Islands, rich in fruits and flowers. The attractive Polynesian children in the public schools merrily sing about their inviting island home.

Transcribed by Mrs. W. A. Coulter at Tutuila School. Collected by Charles Hofmann and *used with his permission.*

CHINESE LULLABY

Carol McCurdy Dewey
Chinese Tune

Sleepily

1. Wil - lows are ben - ding and mur - muring low,
2. Cheeks like the ro - ses and bright, laugh-ing eyes,

Twi-light grows dim-mer, sun-set tints fade! Mo-ther is near to watch
Lips like the cher-ries, lo-tus bud feet; I love you, my dar-ling, now

o - ver you, dear, Swee-ter than ho - ney, pre-cious as jade.
sleep, lit - tle pearl, Bye-low, my lit-tle one, bye - low, my sweet.

The author of the poem and her husband have been in China since 1921.

Words from *Chinese Life Rhythms*, by Carol McCurdy Dewey, *by permission of the author.*
Music contributed by Bliss Wiant.

FAT BABY SISTER

Chinese
Translated by Grace Boynton

Chinese Folk Song
Arranged by Bliss Wiant

Animato

My house has a fat ba-by wee. Not one year is she, Cute as she can be. Won't eat rice, can't drink tea, Nur-ses dai-ly with glee. Wears a wool-ly cap, Coat of pink, you see. When she smiles and coos Like a flower is she. Grand-pa, grand-ma, bro-ther, sis-ter, all love ba-by wee.

Wo chia yu ke p'ang wa wa. Pu tao yi sheng jih, Ling li hui suo hua. Pu ch'ih fan, pu he ch'a, T'ien t'ien ch'ih ma ma. T'ou tai hsiao yang mao, Shen ch'uan fen hung sha. Suo hua lien tai hsiao Hao tz'u hai t'ang hua. Ke ke, ti ti, chieh chieh, mei mei, jen jen tou ai t'a.

"This version is popular in Peking. The romanization of the Chinese characters is the one officially recognized by the Chinese government. The word *pu* sounds like *boo*; *ke* like the first part of *gutter* and it means 'older brother'; *ti*, like *dee*, means 'younger brother.'"

Used by permission of Bliss Wiant.

BALLOON SONG

From the Marathi of Manzubal
Translated by Clara L. Seiler

From India
Music Notation by
Emily R. Bissell

Freely, like a chant

CHORUS: See, Oh, see our charming balloon! Sister, let us play with it this

VERSE 1
golden afternoon. It's such fun to watch it going high up in the sky.

VERSE 2
Up and up it goes, Oh, how it loves to fly! In the air it pauses,

hanging there so free! Brother claps his tiny hands,

VERSE 3
Sister laughs with glee. Look again! It's burst! Oh, me! Oh, my!

VERSE 4
After our smiling now we cry. My Brother, dear, don't

[62]

feel too sad; I'll get you a new one bet-ter than you had.

A singing game, written for children by an Indian poet, from a book of Marathi kindergarten songs. A little girl with her small brother plays with a balloon. She comforts him when the small balloon bursts and he cries.

Used by permission of Emily R. Bissell.

CONGO LULLABY

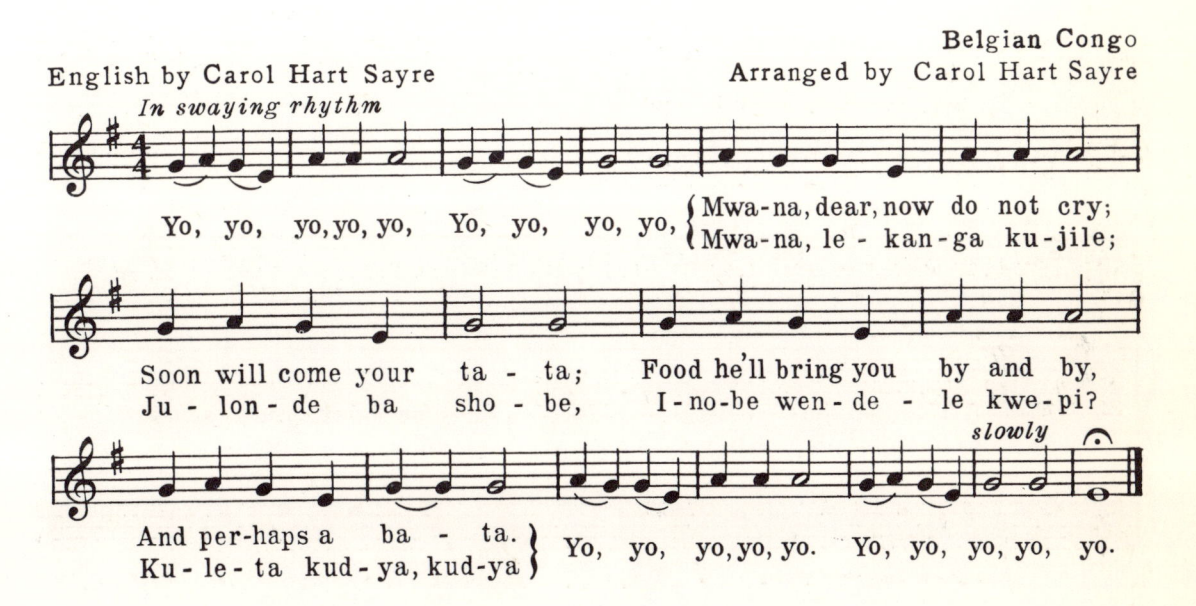

English by Carol Hart Sayre

Belgian Congo
Arranged by Carol Hart Sayre

In swaying rhythm

Yo, yo, yo, yo, yo, Yo, yo, yo, yo, {Mwa-na, dear, now do not cry;
Mwa-na, le-kan-ga ku-jile;

Soon will come your ta - ta; Food he'll bring you by and by,
Ju - lon-de ba sho - be, I-no-be wen-de-le kwe-pi?

slowly

And per-haps a ba - ta.} Yo, yo, yo, yo, yo. Yo, yo, yo, yo, yo.
Ku - le-ta kud-ya, kud-ya

Whatever continent one visits, one finds mothers singing their babies to sleep. This simple lullaby from the Luba tribe of the Belgian Congo is sung by the mothers when tucking their babies under the blankets at night. Here is the meaning of the unfamiliar words: *mwana*—baby; *tata*—father; *bata*—duck.

Used by permission of Carol Hart Sayre.

MY DOLL

Free Paraphrase of the Japanese
Japanese Folk Song

Quietly, slowly

(May be sung unaccompanied)

Ning-yo, you're a love-ly doll, With eyes that o-pen wide,
Wa-ta-shi no ning-yo wa yo-i ning-yo,

Ti-ny mouth, shi-ning teeth,— You're my joy and pride!
Me wa pac-chi-ri to ir-o-ji-o de

Now I'm sing-ing you grow slee-py, I will rock you, so!
Chi-i-sa-i ku-chi-mo-to ai ra-shi-i

If I leave you all a-lone, I'll come back, you know.
Wa-ta-shi no ning-yo wa yo-i ning-yo.

    A Japanese girl in New York sang this doll's lullaby remembered from childhood. In Japan the Doll Festival for girls is held on the third of March every year. In each home the dolls are arranged on shelves in the best room of the house. Girls serve tea to visitors with gentle courtesy.

As sung by Mariko Mukai in New York City and recorded by Charles Hofmann and Louise Morgan.

[64]

MY HOMELAND

Paraphrase of the Swedish

Till Österland
Swedish Folk Song

Not too fast, with feeling

We long to go to the home-land, The place where our fa-thers were born, Where mid-night sun and the moon-light The fo-rests in beau-ty a-dorn. Oh, to be where moun-tains to - wer, And to look on the lin-dens in flower!

"Till Österland" is a Swedish phrase for "land to the East," and it refers to a very beautiful part of the Swedish countryside. Swedish families in America often sing the song and picture in imagination returning to their native land and the joy of homecoming.

As recorded in Washington, D. C., by Charles Hofmann.

MY COUNTRY IS THE WORLD

Robert Whitaker

America
Thesaurus Musicus, 1740

With spirit

1. My country is the world; My flag with stars im-pearled
2. Mine are all lands and seas, All flowers, shrubs, and trees,
3. And all men are my kin, Since ever man has been

Fills all the skies. All the round earth I claim, Peoples of
All life's design. My heart within me thrills For all up-
Blood of my blood; I glory in the grace And strength of

every name, And all inspiring fame, My heart would prize.
lifted hills, And for all streams and rills; The world is mine.
every race, And joy in every trace Of brotherhood.

Robert Whitaker believed that he belonged not only to his native America but to the whole world. He stated this belief in lines to be sung to the tune that Americans, English, and Danes use for their national hymn. Mr. Whitaker held his conviction so firmly during World War I that he went to prison rather than take up arms against any brother.

Words used by permission of Mrs. Robert Whitaker.

: 5 :

WATCH AND WONDER

*This is the doing of the Eternal—
we can but watch and wonder.*

—Psalms 118:23

SECTION FIVE
SUGGESTIONS FOR SINGING

Sounds That Make Us Glad, page 71. A group of juniors were singing in "The Rain Song" about the "slender, silvery drumsticks" of the rain. The musical sound set them to thinking of and mentioning pleasures that come through the ear. You can guess that they were country children by reading the sounds they like. Arranging the ideas in a litany, a responsive order of appreciations, they alternated the paragraphs they made up with a sentence they found in *Psalms* 4: 7 to show who is the One who makes us glad. The words were lifted into music, chanted brightly on a high tone. The piano played chords to support it, and one of the boys added a little higher tune on his violin for a bird's call. Making this kind of poem together is a good way for any group to pray aloud. Try it!

Pippa's Song, page 72. This is the one song in the book that really needs two-part singing to bring out the full beauty of the music and the joy of a singing heart poured out in poetry.

Shiny Little Moon, page 74. The children may pretend that they are Greek children going to school secretly by night. Two hundred years ago when Greece was held by conquerors, the boys and girls were not allowed to attend school openly.

FOR CHILDREN

G. W. Briggs

St. Columba
Irish Hymn Tune

Flowing

1. I love God's tiny creatures That wander wild and free,— The coral-coated ladybird, The velvet humming bee.
2. Shy little flowers in hedge and dyke, That hide themselves away: God paints them, though they are so small, God makes them bright and gay.

"Look at the birds of the air: ... your heavenly Father feeds them. Are you not of more value than they? ... Consider the lilies of the field, how they grow; ... if God so clothes the grass of the field, ... will he not much more clothe you ... ?" (*Matthew* 6: 26, 28, 30. Revised Standard Version.)

Words from *Songs of Faith*, by permission of the Oxford University Press, London.

EASTER SURPRISES

Edith Lovell Thomas

German Folk Song
Arranged by Brahms for
the Schumann Children

Slowly, rhythmically

1. Out of an egg comes a sing-ing bird; Out of a seed comes a flower; Dark of the night turns to mor-ning light; Clouds turn to snow or to shower.
2. Look for the won-ders of Ea-ster-time, Won-ders that A-pril will bring. O-pen your eyes for a new sur-prise! God is at work in the spring.

The spirit of springtime can be felt in the music of this German folk song of "The Nightingale."

[70]

SOUNDS THAT MAKE US GLAD

Psalms 4: 7

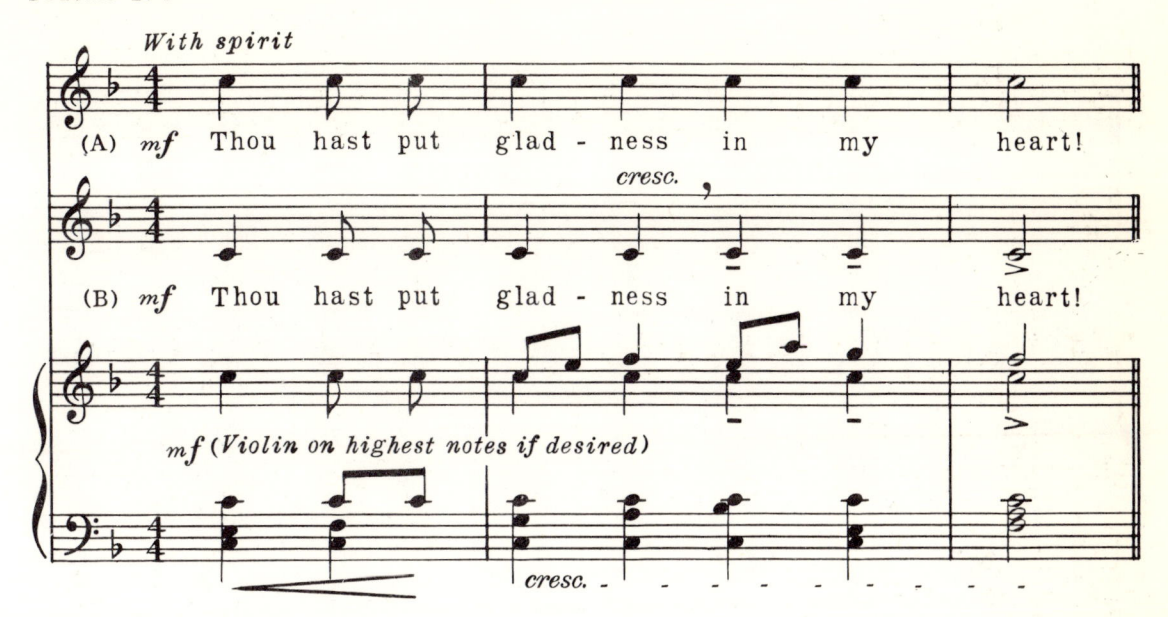

With spirit

(A) *mf* Thou hast put glad-ness in my heart!

(B) *mf* Thou hast put glad-ness in my heart!

mf (Violin on highest notes if desired)

LEADER
We thank thee for the sounds we hear:
The birds singing in the early morning;
GROUP (singing MUSICAL RESPONSE)

[Use (A) or (B) or both together as preferred.]

LEADER
The rooster crowing at dawn;
The voices of the owls hooting at night;
The katydids singing, "Katydid, katydid, katydid!" (RESPONSE)

LEADER
The babbling brook, running over pebbles;
The waterfall, swishing over the rocks;
The rain, falling like silver drumsticks; (RESPONSE)

LEADER
The faraway sound of the train at night;
The faint sound of the deer's footsteps going through the bushes;
The wind whistling in the treetops;
The sound of the children's voices singing with the violin. (RESPONSE)

Junior Class, Laboratory School, Carmel, New York, July, 1945, under the guidance of Mary Esther McWhirter. *Used by permission of Mrs. McWhirter.*

PIPPA'S SONG

Robert Browning William G. Hammond

Con spirito

The year's at the spring, And day's at the morn; Morning's at seven; The hill-side's dew-pearled; The lark's on the wing; The

The year's at the spring, And day's at the morn; Morning's at seven; The hill-side's dew-pearled; The lark's on the wing; The snail's on the thorn; God's in his heaven— All's right with the world!

snail's on the thorn; God's in his hea-ven—All's right with the world!

Pippa, an Italian girl, works in a silk mill and has only one holiday in the entire year. On that day she is full of joy and she goes around the town singing this song of praise to God for his wonderful world. Wherever Pippa passes, there goes the song of a child calling attention to the loveliness around her.

From *The Progressive Music Series*, Book Three, copyright 1916, *by special permission of the authors and publishers*, Silver Burdett Company, New York.

SHINY LITTLE MOON

English Version by
Helen Vyronis Halley

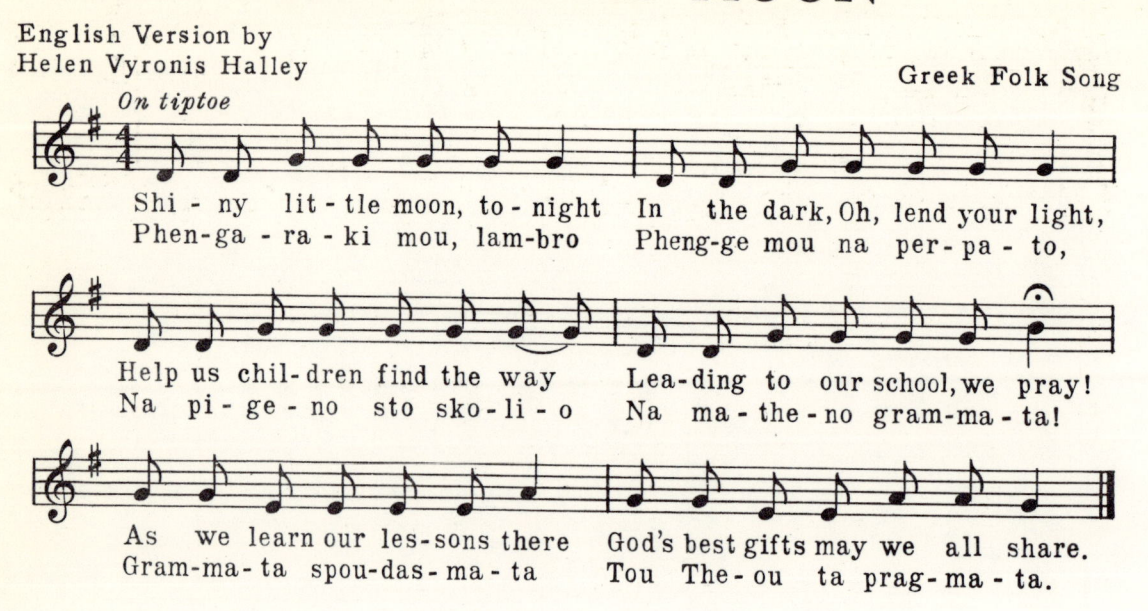

Greek Folk Song

On tiptoe

Shi - ny lit - tle moon, to - night In the dark, Oh, lend your light,
Phen - ga - ra - ki mou, lam - bro Pheng - ge mou na per - pa - to,

Help us chil - dren find the way Lea - ding to our school, we pray!
Na pi - ge - no sto sko - li - o Na ma - the - no gram - ma - ta!

As we learn our les - sons there God's best gifts may we all share.
Gram - ma - ta spou - das - ma - ta Tou The - ou ta prag - ma - ta.

As sung by Helen Vyronis Halley. Collected by Charles Hofmann in New York City and *used with his permission.*

FIREFLY

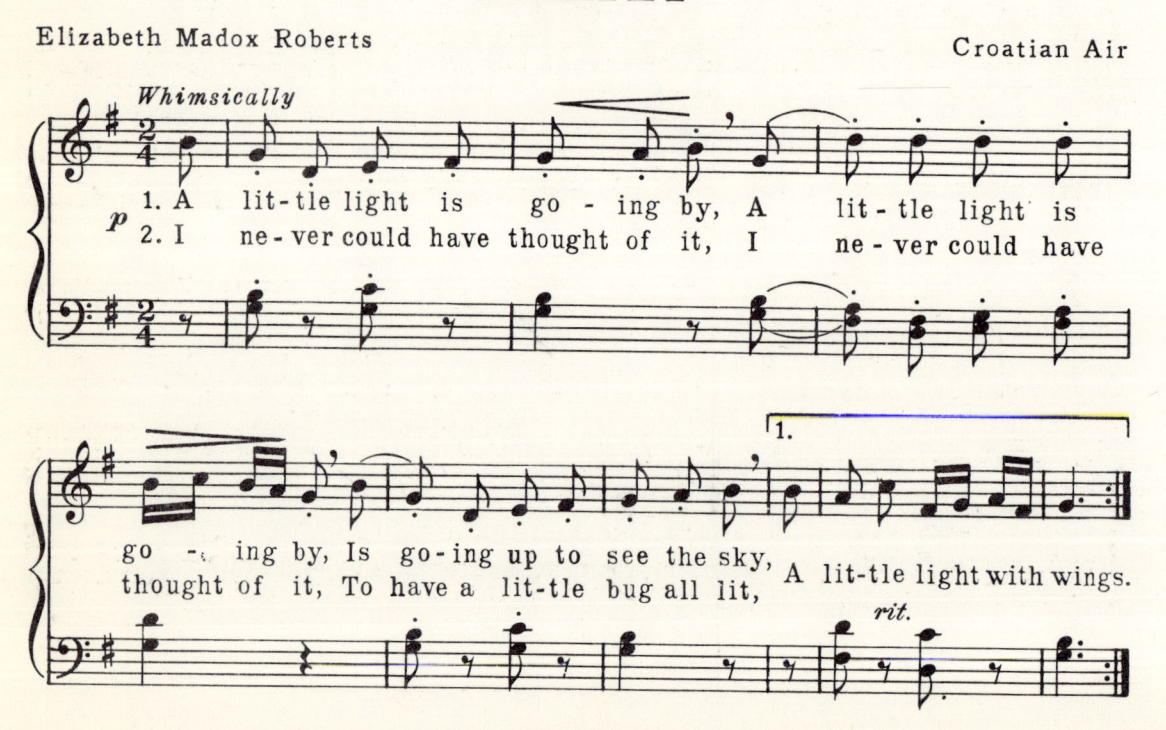

Elizabeth Madox Roberts

Croatian Air

Whimsically

1. A lit - tle light is go - ing by, A lit - tle light is
2. I ne - ver could have thought of it, I ne - ver could have

go - ing by, Is go - ing up to see the sky, A lit - tle light with wings.
thought of it, To have a lit - tle bug all lit,

rit.

[74]

And made to go on wings, on wings.

p *pp*

Words from *Under the Tree*, by Elizabeth Madox Roberts. Copyright, 1922, by B. W. Huebsch. *Reprinted by permission of The Viking Press, Inc., New York.*

BRIGHT MOON

Hallie Buie Korean Air

With hushed excitement

1. Come and see What is here! Moon is bright-ly bea - ming.
2. Moun-tain high, Wa - ter deep, Eve-ry place a - dor - ning

On the world Shi-ning clear, Like a lamp it's glea - ming.
Near-by plain, Hill-side steep, Moon-light paints like mor - ning!

Used by permission of Virginia Fairfax.

HIGH IS THE BLUE SKY

Paraphrase of the Chinese
Chinese Folk Song

Strongly accented

High and blue the sky; Trees are ve-ry tall;
Tsing ti-en kao, Yuan shu shee,

Wild geese fly-ing seem so small. See! on si-lent wings in
See foong chee, yen chuing fee. Fee tso ee tze

flocks they go, Ne-ver par-ting from the sin-gle row!
ee han chee, Fee lai fee chu boo femg lee,

We go hand in hand, Like the wild geese band: Bro-thers are we strong and free.
Hao siang wo, Guh guh dee dee, Siang tsing siang ai shou siang shee.

Contributed to Charles Hofmann collection by Liu Liang-mo and *used with their permission.* English version by Liu Liang-mo and Donna Nichols.

BACK OF THE BREAD

Maltbie D. Babcock
Text Altered

Peter Christian Lutkin

Gently swaying

Back of the bread is the snow-y flour; Back of the flour is the mill;

Back of the mill the gro-wing wheat Nods on the bree-zy hill;

O-ver the wheat is the glo-wing sun, Rip'-ning the heart of the grain; A-

bove the sun is the gra-cious God, Sen-ding the sun-light and rain.

The author of this poem was thinking one day of the phrase from the Lord's Prayer: "Give us this day our daily bread." He thought of the work of the baker, the farmer, and the miller, and of God's gifts that helped the grain to grow. He put his thoughts together in a poem.

From *The Progressive Music Series*, Book Three, copyright 1916, *by special permission of the authors and publishers, Silver Burdett Company, New York.*

WHAT DO WE PLANT

Henry Abbey French Melody

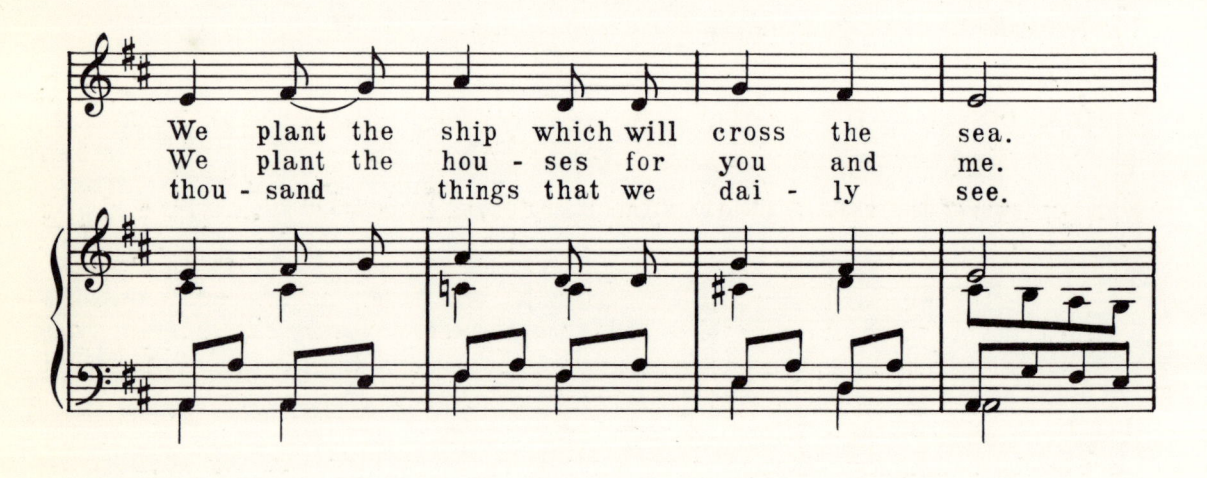

Sturdily

1. What do we plant when we plant a tree?
2. What do we plant when we plant a tree?
3. What do we plant when we plant a tree? A

We plant the ship which will cross the sea.
We plant the hou-ses for you and me.
thou-sand things that we dai-ly see.

We plant the mast to car-ry the sails;
We plant the raf-ters, the shin-gles, the floors;
We plant the spire that out-to-wers the crag;

We plant the planks to with-stand the gales; The
We plant the stud-ding, the lath, the doors; The
We plant the staff for our coun-try's flag; We

keel, the keel-son, the beam, the knee:
beams, the si-ding,—all parts that be:
plant the shade, from the hot sun free:

All these we plant when we plant a tree.

Anyone who has planted a seed and watched it turn into a plant knows something of the mystery of growing things. We wonder how a tiny seed buried in the soil can be changed into "a thousand things that we daily see."

Words from *The Poems of Henry Abbey*, published by D. Appleton, 1904. *By permission of D. Appleton-Century Company, Inc., New York.*

A THANKSGIVING

John Kendrick Bangs George H. Gartlan

Moderato

1. For sum-mer rain and win-ter's sun, For au-tumn bree-zes crisp and sweet; For la-bors do-ing, to be done, And la-bors all com-plete; For A-pril, May and love-ly June, For bud and bird and ber-ried vine, For

2. For light and air, for sun and shade, For mer-ry laugh-ter and for cheer; For mu-sic and the glad pa-rade Of bles-sings through the year; For all the fruit-ful earth's in-crease, For home and life and love di-vine, For

[80]

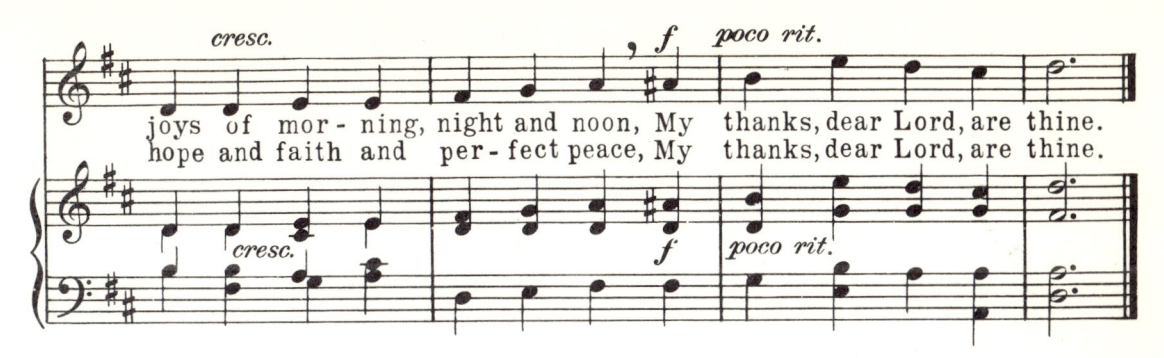

joys of mor-ning, night and noon, My thanks, dear Lord, are thine.
hope and faith and per-fect peace, My thanks, dear Lord, are thine.

*From Universal Song Book, by Damrosch, Gartlan and Gehrkens.
Used by permission of the publishers, Hinds, Hayden & Eldredge, Inc.*

HAPPY NEW YEAR

Katherine Edelman

Melody by Agathe Backer-Gröndal

Briskly

A hap-py New Year For you, for me, For friend, for stran-ger A-cross the sea; For the po-lice-man U-pon our beat, And for the boy and girl A-cross the street.

Words used by permission of the author.

[81]

PARTNERS

Edwin Markham
Smoothly and rather slowly

Pretty Polly Oliver
English Air

Who digs a well, or plants a seed, A sa-cred pact he keeps with sun and sod; With these he helps re-fresh and feed The world, and en-ters in-to part-ner-ship with God.

Words reprinted by permission.

:6:

DAYS OF JOY

*God...richly provides us
with all the enjoyments of life.*

—I Timothy 6: 17

SECTION SIX
SUGGESTIONS FOR SINGING

From Heaven High, page 90. Dr. Roland Bainton writes of this hymn: "The carol is designed for a children's pageant in the church. Before the altar is placed a cradle with the Babe. On either side kneel Mary and Joseph. From the choir a chorister takes the part of the angel and makes the announcement: 'From heaven high I come to earth. I bring you tidings of great mirth.' The shepherds and the children in the meantime have been standing just below the chancel steps. 'Look now, you children, at the sign' is their cue. At the close of this stanza the children take up the song, 'How glad we'll be if it is so! With all the shepherds let us go.' Singing they come forward around the cradle, and in unison or singly take up the stanzas that exclaim over the Baby Jesus and invite him to be guest in their hearts. The closing stanza is sung by all, angels, shepherds, children, and the entire audience." (From *The Martin Luther Christmas Book,* by Roland Bainton, The Westminster Press, 1948.) In your church or at home you might enjoy doing this very famous old carol in dramatic form.

A Christmas Antiphon, page 93. A leader sings each line, and then the chorus repeats that line and adds the two following lines, "We love Christmas dearly; We love Christmas Day," each time. The music goes rather quickly.

Christmas in Mexico, pages 94 and 95. In Mexico people like to act out these songs. Neighbors and their families join in procession on the evening of December sixteenth and the nine nights succeeding. Two children lead the procession, bearing on a litter small figures to represent Mary on a burro, Joseph, and an angel. The company of neighbors, each holding a lighted candle, moves to a particular house where the first *posada* (page 94) is sung. The head of the house refuses them admittance, but when he is persuaded of how important they are, the inn-keeper and his family invite them in with the second *posada* (page 95). Entering, they kneel and say together the "Ave Maria" and "Our Father." Next comes a good time with games, eating, and dancing. Every night in a different home this ceremony takes place. The children might enjoy acting out the songs.

MERRY CHRISTMAS

Frances E. Jacobs　　　　　　　　　　　　　　　　　　　　　　　　J. A. P. Schulz

Allegro non troppo

Yes, Christ-mas is co-ming, How hap-py the day! We wish "Mer-ry Christ-mas" to those far a-way: "Ein fröh-li-ches Weih-nach-ten," "Jo-yeux No-ël," And "Buon Na-ta-le," The same gree-tings tell.

This little song gives us the words that German, French, and Italian people use when they wish their friends "Merry Christmas."

From *Old Tunes with New Rhymes*, by Frances E. Jacobs, published and copyrighted (1931) by Oliver Ditson Company.

MIGHTY DAY

Negro Spiritual

Moderato

Was-n't that a migh-ty day? Hal-le-lu! Hal-le-lu-jah! Was-n't that a migh-ty day When Je-sus Christ was born?

This Negro spiritual is a musical exclamation over the wonder of the coming of Jesus into the world to bring hope, freedom, and joy to all mankind.

A JOYFUL THING

Translated from the French
by Rev. J. O'Connor (Alt.)

Besançon Noël

In lively spirit

1. We've been told a joy-ful thing, News for all the na-tions.
2. Up and get you quick-ly there, Folk of field and vil-lage!

Angels have been heard to sing Round the shep-herd sta - tions,
O - ver to that sta - ble bare, Up be-yond the til - lage.

One in-toned the GLO-RI - A, O - thers, AL - LE - LU - I - A.
There you'll find a Ba - by born, With his mo-ther in the morn,

Peace on earth, good will to men; War no more the world shall fill.
Sing to - ge - ther "Glo - ri - a!" Sing your "Al - le - lu - i - a!"

"Alleluia" is the Latin for the Hebrew word "Hallelujah" and means "Praise ye the Lord." "Gloria" is the Latin way of saying "glory." In the song the shepherds are telling the story of how they heard the angels sing and what their message was.

From *Carols, Customs and Costumes around the World*, compiled by Herbert H. Wernecke. By permission of The Old Orchard Publishers, Webster Groves, Missouri.

LULLABY TO THE CHRIST CHILD

Arousiag Donigian
Text Altered

Armenian Folk Melody

Very quietly

1. Sleep, my ba-by, my be-lo-ved, Lul-la-by I sing,
2. Sleep, my ba-by, Ho-ly In-fant, Hope of Is-ra-el;

While the moon, so soft-ly shi-ning, Rest to you will bring.
Now the world with joy is sing-ing! Sleep, E-ma-nu-el.

An Armenian Junior College student has given us this lovely song used by his people for long years. As a country, Armenia was the very first to adopt the Christian faith. The word "Emanuel" is Hebrew and means "God with us." It is one of the many names for Jesus that tells something of what he means to people.

THE LITTLE JESUS
(El Niño Jesus)

Paraphrase of the Spanish — Puerto Rican Folk Melody

Gently

Come, shep-herds, come to Beth-le-hem to-day!
See there a boy who rests u-pon the hay!
Come, eve-ry-one, be-hold and me-di-tate:
Will he be King for all to ve-ne-rate?

Ve - nid, ve - nid, pas - to - res sin tar - dar!
Al San - to Rey, Je - sus a con-tem-plar.
Ve - nid, ve - nid, al ni - ño a a - do - rar.
Ve - nid, ve - nid, al Rey a ve - ne - rar.

A shepherd's song, or "pastoral," that comes from rhythm-loving Spain is one that might be heard as it is played on flutelike pipes.

As recorded in Tampa, Florida, by Charles Hofmann.

FROM HEAVEN HIGH

Martin Luther
Translated by Roland H. Bainton
Abbreviated

Vom Himmel Hoch
Martin Luther, 1539

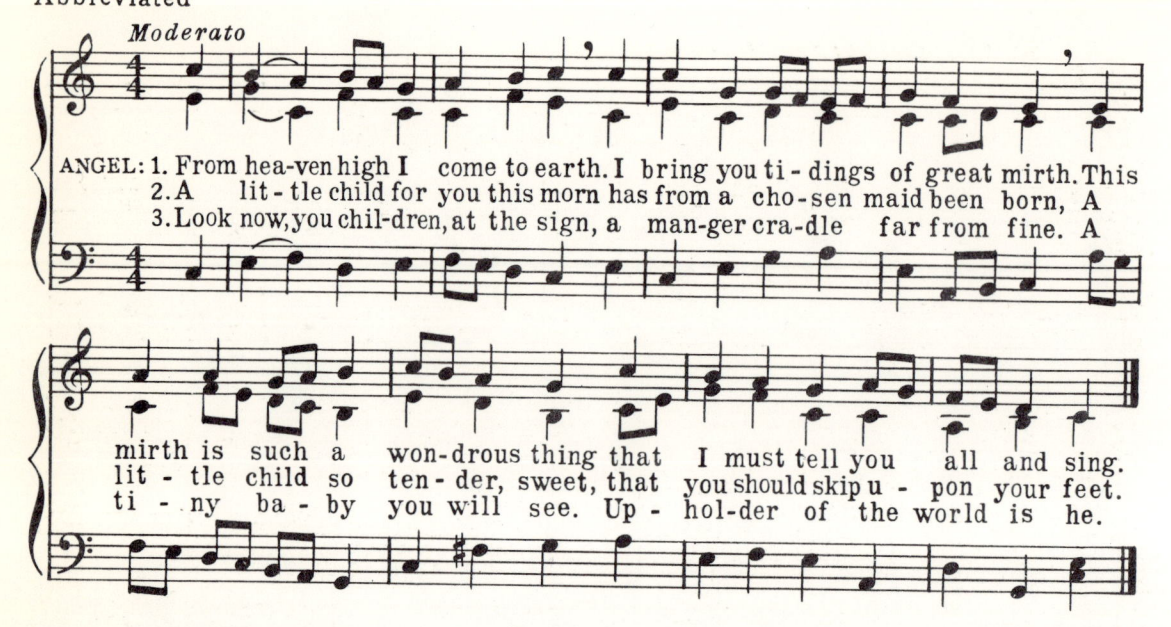

ANGEL:
1. From heaven high I come to earth. I bring you tidings of great mirth. This mirth is such a wondrous thing that I must tell you all and sing.
2. A little child for you this morn has from a chosen maid been born, A little child so tender, sweet, that you should skip upon your feet.
3. Look now, you children, at the sign, a manger cradle far from fine. A tiny baby you will see. Upholder of the world is he.

CHILDREN
4. How glad we'll be if it is so! With all the shepherds let us go
   To see what God for us has done in sending us his own dear Son.

5. Look, look, my heart, and let me peek. Whom in the manger do you seek?
   Who is that lovely little one? The Baby Jesus, God's own Son.

6. Be welcome, Lord; be now our guest. By you poor sinners have been blessed.
   In nakedness and cold you lie. How can I thank you — how can I?

7. O dear Lord Jesus, for your head now will I make the softest bed.
   The chamber where this bed shall be is in my heart, inside of me.

8. I can play the whole day long. I'll dance and sing for you a song,
   A soft and soothing lullaby, so sweet that you will never cry.

ALL
9. To God who sent his only Son be glory, laud, and honor done.
   Let all the choir of heaven rejoice, sing "Glad New Year" with heart and voice.

From *The Martin Luther Christmas Book*, by Roland Bainton, The Westminster Press, 1948.
Used by permission of author and publishers.

MARY'S LULLABY

Translated from the Japanese by Willis Lamott
Paraphrased by Edith Lovell Thomas

Adapted from the Japanese Air

Smoothly rocking movement

p On the hay in the sta-ble Ba-by Je-sus lies; *mp* Mo-ther Ma-ry soft-ly sings, "Eve-ning time, close your eyes.

p Sil-ver stars, a-bove the cold earth, Shine u-pon your bed;

ritenuto

p In the dark night you may rest, While they watch o-ver-head."

Copyright, 1950, by Friendship Press.

THE CHRIST CHILD'S STABLE

Ida Tyson Wagner

The Star
Alsatian Folk Song

Lightly, not too slowly

1. The stable was old and rude and bare! Yet two poor folks found shelter there; And for a Babe without a toy No inn could ever hold such joy. For there were woolly lambs, a small Brown donkey by the oxen's stall.
2. A silken web a spider spread In lacy pattern overhead; A soft gray dove, with coral feet, That closed his eyes with cooing sweet. And when a star peeked down at night, I know he loved its twinkling light.

The Christ Child was born in a stable, and yet, even in that humble spot there were riches to enjoy—the presence of animals, the silken web of a spider, a dove, the light of a star, and his parents' love.

Artists, poets, storytellers, and musicians through the ages have taken pleasure in trying to picture the stable scene the night that Jesus was born.

Words from *Children's Religion*. Copyright, The Pilgrim Press.
Used by permission.

A CHRISTMAS ANTIPHON

Arranged from the African

African
From Jessie B. Terril

Joyously

LEADER: 1. Je - sus Christ was born on Christ - mas.
2. Ma - ry was his love - ly mo - ther.

CHORUS: Je - sus Christ was born on Christ - mas.
Ma - ry was his love - ly mo - ther.

1 & 2. We love Christ-mas dear-ly; We love Christ-mas Day.

This antiphonal way of singing, when leader and group take turns, is a common African custom. It is often used while work is being done or stories are told. It comes from the Tswa language of the Bantu people.

Used by permission of Jessie B. Terril.

CHRISTMAS IN MEXICO

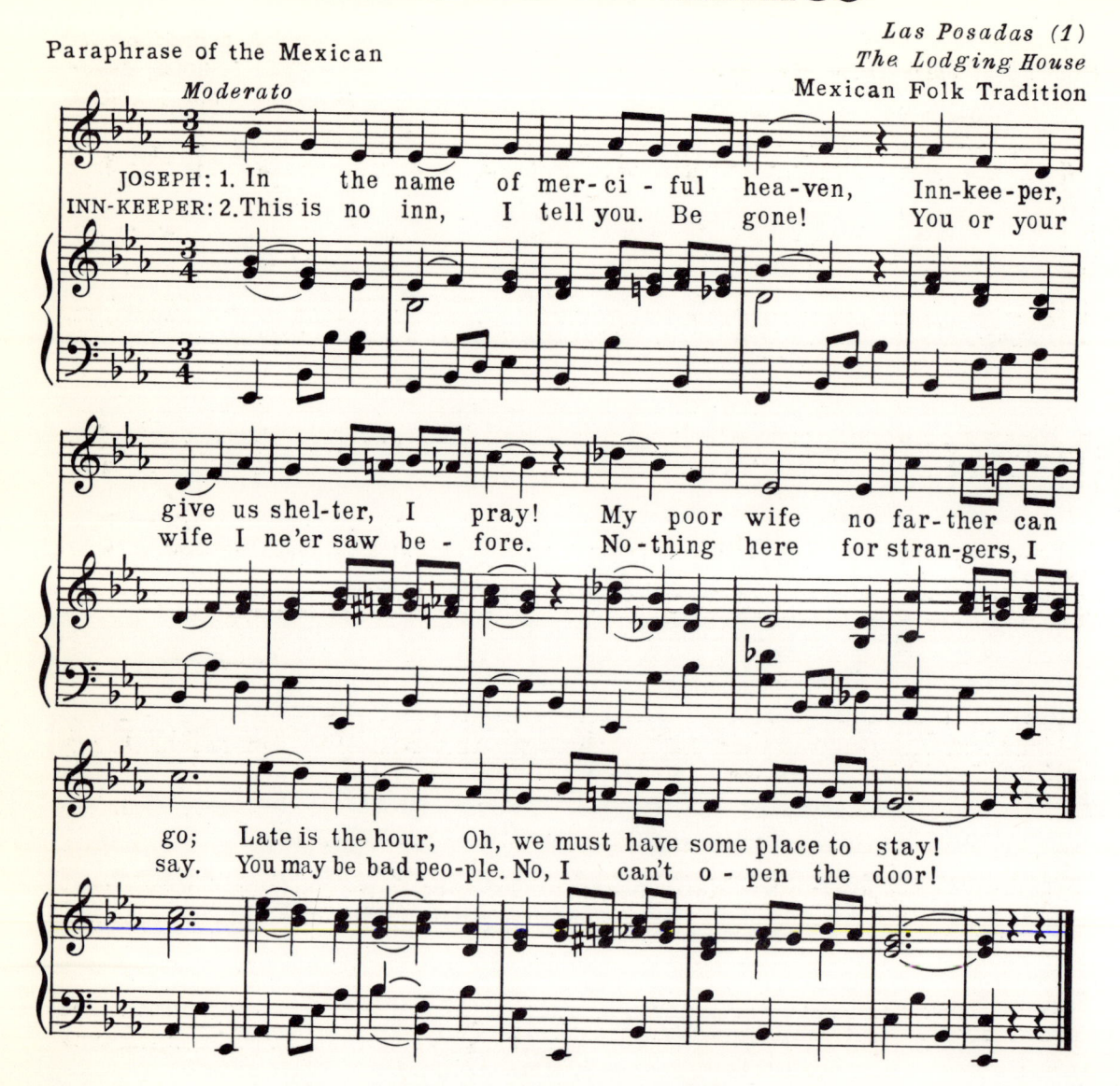

Paraphrase of the Mexican

Las Posadas (1)
The Lodging House
Mexican Folk Tradition

Moderato

JOSEPH: 1. In the name of mer-ci-ful hea-ven, Inn-kee-per, give us shel-ter, I pray! My poor wife no far-ther can go; Late is the hour, Oh, we must have some place to stay!

INN-KEEPER: 2. This is no inn, I tell you. Be gone! You or your wife I ne'er saw be-fore. No-thing here for stran-gers, I say. You may be bad peo-ple. No, I can't o-pen the door!

JOSEPH: 3. Please be kind to us! Oh, have pity!
We are so tired. A long way we came.
Our good Lord reward will give you.
I am the village carpenter, Joseph, by name.

INN-KEEPER: 4. You are Joseph? I did not know you!
So you come here with Mary, your wife?
Here's a room. A welcome indeed!
Enter, pilgrims. Share with us all of our life!

CHRISTMAS IN MEXICO

Free Paraphrase of the Mexican

Las Posadas (2)
The Lodging House
Mexican Folk Tradition

Heartily

1. Let the doors fly open wide to way-worn pilgrims, Who for comfort seek within! Here is rest for traveling strangers, food for the hungry, Sleep for weary ones to win.

2. Peace to you, O holy pilgrims! We pray, enter, Make our home your dwelling place. Not alone to this poor lodging lend a blessing— With our hearts Oh, share your grace!

Both songs recorded by Charles Hofmann. Copyright, 1940 and 1946.
Used by permission.

[95]

BIRTHDAY PRESENTS

Paraphrase of the Japanese

Translated from the Japanese by Willis Lamott
Paraphrased by Edith Lovell Thomas

Lightly

1. Cup of warm milk, Ba - by Je - sus,
   Pre - sent from the Cow; She has given it
   for your birth-day. Drink it, drink it now!

2. Wool - ly blan - ket, Ba - by Je - sus,
   Pre - sent from the Sheep; It will be a
   soft, white co - ver When you go to sleep.

3. If you're hun - gry, Ba - by Je - sus,
   What will you eat then? Taste this brown egg,
   you will like it, Brought by Mo - ther Hen.

4. Here's another present, Jesus,
       When you want some fun:
     On his back the Colt will take you
       Riding in the sun.

Copyright, 1950, by Friendship Press.

CHANUKAH

Translated from the Hebrew of L. Kipnis
by Rabbi Jerome R. Malino

Chanukah
Jewish Folk Song

Lively

1. Cha-nu-kah, Cha-nu-kah, Fe-sti-val of fun, Light, so soft,
2. Cha-nu-kah, Cha-nu-kah, Lights burn eve-ry-where, Pan-cake treat,

Shine a-loft__ Joy for eve-ry-one. Cha-nu-kah, Cha-nu-kah,
Cakes to eat, Eve-ry home will share. Cha-nu-kah, Cha-nu-kah,

Tops spin mer-ri-ly, Spin, spin, spin, Spin, spin, spin, Gai-ly as can be.
Hap-py ho-li-day, Let us play, Let us sing, Let us dance a-way!

The Jewish people in December keep a very ancient celebration known as "The Feast of Lights," or "Chanukah." Candles are burned for eight days in synagogues and homes. Parties and entertainments are enjoyed. The feast celebrates the purification of the Temple at Jerusalem after a pagan altar had been set up within it by a foreign invader.

Adapted from *Songs of Zion,* compiled and edited by Harry Coopersmith, Behrman House, Inc., Publishers, New York.

ST. VALENTINE'S DAY

Ophelia's Song
William Shakespeare

Eighteenth Century English Tune

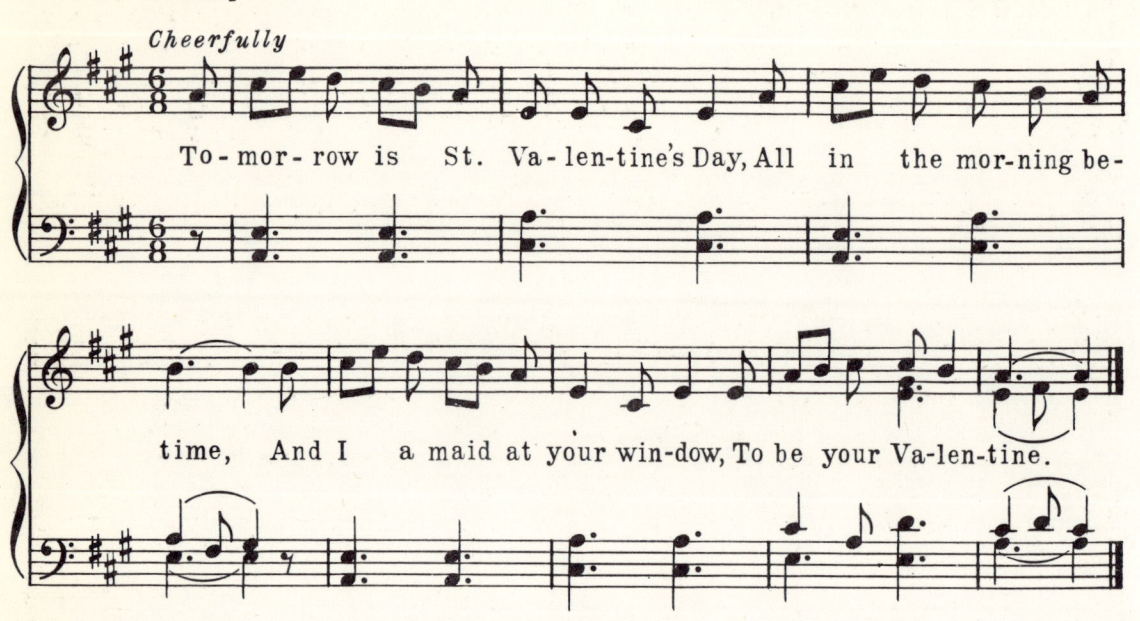

Cheerfully

To-mor-row is St. Va-len-tine's Day, All in the mor-ning be-time, And I a maid at your win-dow, To be your Va-len-tine.

THE FIRST COURIER

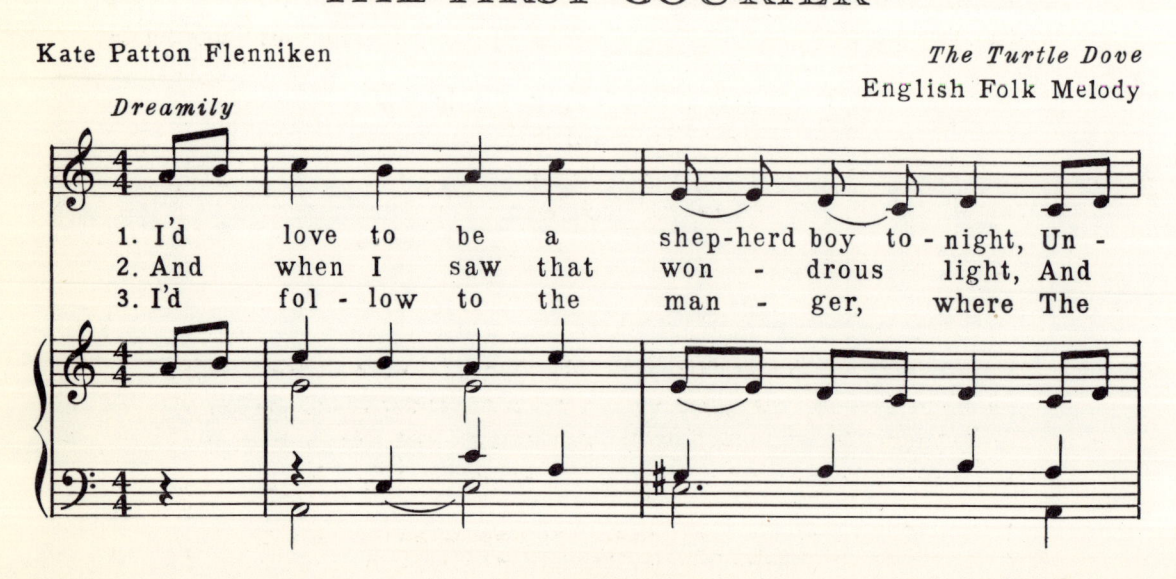

Kate Patton Flenniken

The Turtle Dove
English Folk Melody

Dreamily

1. I'd love to be a shep-herd boy to-night, Un-
2. And when I saw that won-drous light, And
3. I'd fol-low to the man-ger, where The

der the o-pen sky: I'd herd my sheep, and then I'd watch The
heard the an-gels' song,   I'd hast-en in-to Beth-le-hem Be-
lit-tle Je-sus lay: I'd drop my crook and wal-let down, So

shi-ning stars go by, The shi-ning stars go by.
hind the shi-ning throng, Be-hind the shi-ning throng.
I could kneel and pray, So I could kneel and pray.

4. But I would have no gift that I
    Could offer to a King,
  Since just a bit of fish and bread
    Was all I had to bring.

5. But I would speed with flying feet
    To wake that sleeping town,
  And lead them to the manger, where
    The new born babe was found.

6. And then we'd hurry in to kneel
    Upon the sanded floor,
  While overhead the great white star
    Lit up the stable door.

The poet imagines what it would be like to have been a shepherd boy at Bethlehem the night that Jesus was born. The words of the song picture what the boy would do. Imagine yourself as the first messenger or "courier" to reach the little Jesus. What gift would you bring?

Words used by permission of Margaret Ansley Flenniken. Melody recorded in Brooklyn, New York, by Charles Hofmann. Used by permission.

ALL GLORY, LAUD, AND HONOR

St. Theodulph, about 820
Translated by John Mason Neale, 1854

St. Theodulph
Melchior Teschner, 1615

As a march

REFRAIN
{ All glo-ry, laud, and ho-nor To thee, Re-dee-mer, King!
To whom the lips of chil-dren Made sweet ho-san-nas ring.

1. The peo-ple of the He-brews With palms be-fore thee went;
2. To thee, be-fore thy Pas-sion, They sang their hymns of praise;
3. Thou didst ac-cept their prai-ses; Ac-cept the prayers we bring,

Our praise and prayer and an-thems Be-fore thee we pre-sent.
To thee, now high ex-al-ted, Our me-lo-dy we raise.
Who in all good de-ligh-test, Thou good and gra-cious King.

Refrain before and after each stanza D.C.

Every Palm Sunday this famous hymn is sung as a choir processional in Catholic and Protestant churches. The poem was composed in Latin in the ninth century by a French bishop and joined to a marching German tune in the seventeenth century.

:7:

TOGETHER IN WORSHIP

Have we not all one Father?

has not one God made us?

—Malachi 2: 10a

SECTION SEVEN
SUGGESTIONS FOR SINGING

Praise and Thanksgiving, page 103. Singing the language of another people instead of our own helps bring us closer to them. If you can find a German person to help with pronunciation, try having the children learn the German words of this song before using the English ones. Sing the song as a round (see directions for "Come Out to Play," page 13), which will give the impression of many peoples offering praise to one Father more realistically than plain unison song can do.

Stories of Jesus, page 110. This is a story hymn that really seems to need pictures to illustrate it. Look up the verses in the New Testament that tell of the incidents mentioned in the story. The children may collect all the pictures they can showing how artists have used their imagination to tell of Jesus, whom they never saw. Show the pictures on a screen, have them put into a book, or use a special one to make a worship center beautiful as the hymn is sung.

Manitou Listens to Me, page 116. One voice singing without accompaniment, the other voices humming, may help the children to picture themselves standing on the mountain with the lone Indian, talking to the Great Spirit.

BEFORE WORSHIP

Second Grade Children
Riverside Church, New York

Second Grade Choir
The Church in Radburn, New Jersey

Slowly

Walk slow-ly, Be si-lent; For this is the place
Where lo-ving and kind-ness Re-mind us of God.

In this little song primary children suggest how to make ready for worship.

Words from *As Children Worship*, by Jeanette E. Perkins. Copyright, The Pilgrim Press.
Used by permission of the author and publisher.

PRAISE AND THANKSGIVING

Paraphrase of the German

Lobet und Preiset
Alsatian Round

Heartily

I. Praise and thanks-gi-ving let eve-ry-one bring Un-to our
Lo-bet und prei-set, ihr Völ-ker den Herrn! Freu-et euch
Fa-ther for eve-ry good thing! All to-ge-ther joy-ful-ly sing!
sei-ner und die-net ihm gern. All' ihr Völ-ker, lo-bet den Herrn!

[103]

THROUGH EVERY LAND

Isaac Watts, Stanza 1, 1719
Stanza 2, Anonymous

Old 100th
Genevan Psalter, 1551

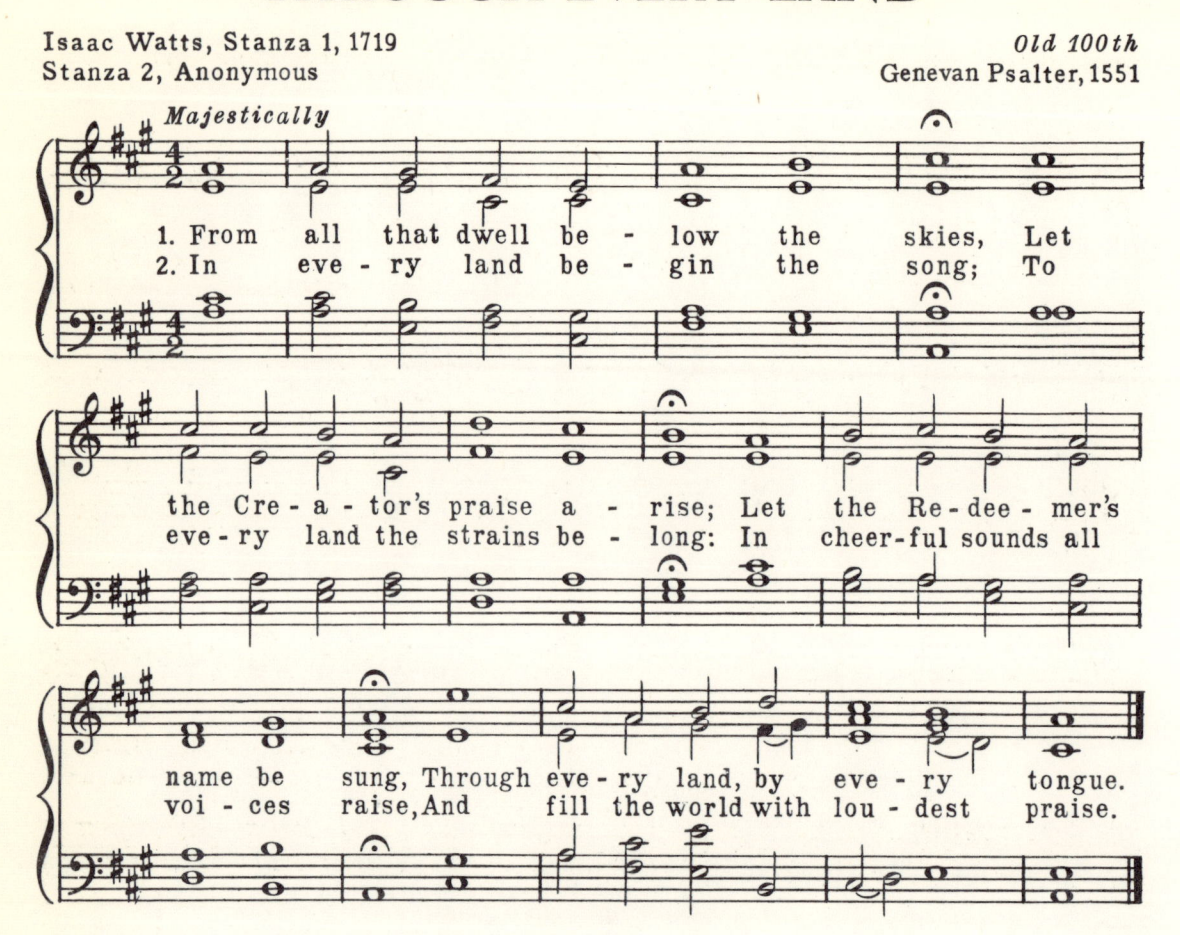

Majestically

1. From all that dwell be-low the skies, Let the Cre-a-tor's praise a-rise; Let the Re-dee-mer's name be sung, Through eve-ry land, by eve-ry tongue.
2. In eve-ry land be-gin the song; To eve-ry land the strains be-long: In cheer-ful sounds all voi-ces raise, And fill the world with lou-dest praise.

ALL PEOPLE
(*Alternate hymn to above tune*)

All people that on earth do dwell,
Sing to the Lord with cheerful voice.
Him serve with mirth, his praise forth tell;
Come ye before him and rejoice.

WILLIAM KETHE

This tune is one of the most beloved and most used of Protestant hymns. It is known as "Old Hundredth" and is sung to a metrical version of Psalm 100. Written for the Genevan Psalter in Switzerland in 1551 it was carried home to England by English religious refugees who had been obliged to flee their own land for a time. William Kethe, writer of another version of the Psalm was one of these refugees. Isaac Watts was one of the first poets to write songs and hymns for children.

O PRAISE YE THE LORD

Paraphrase of *Psalm 150* Theme from César Franck

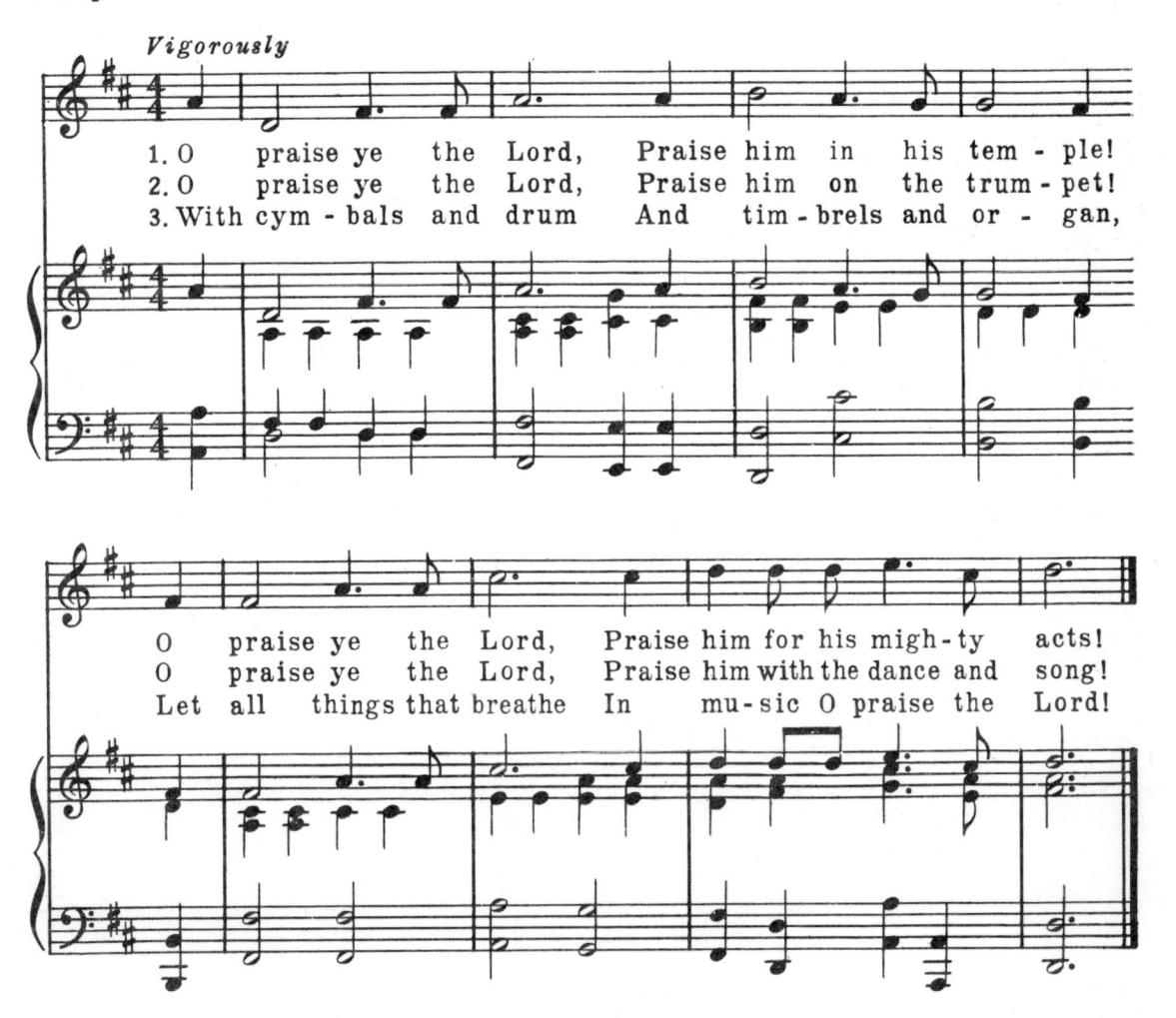

Vigorously

1. O praise ye the Lord, Praise him in his tem-ple!
2. O praise ye the Lord, Praise him on the trum-pet!
3. With cym-bals and drum And tim-brels and or-gan,

O praise ye the Lord, Praise him for his migh-ty acts!
O praise ye the Lord, Praise him with the dance and song!
Let all things that breathe In mu-sic O praise the Lord!

César Franck was a composer-organist in a large Parisian church, and he was a deeply religious man. He wrote a joyous anthem for choir, and this music is a section of it. Psalm 150 is his subject just as it was for Luca della Robbia when he carved figures of players and singers for a choir gallery in Florence, Italy. The psalm, the music, and pictures of the sculptures inspired some children to make up verses about them.

Stanzas 2 and 3 arranged by Junior Vacation School, Richmond Hill Methodist Church, New York, July, 1944.

HOUSES OF WORSHIP

Edith Lovell Thomas
Sustained, deliberate

Charles F. Gounod
Arranged by N. A. Montani

1. Glad-ly to the house of wor-ship come we to-day,
   Thanks to give for qui-et chur-ches where peo-ple pray;
   For the or-gan mu-sic soun-ding far off and near;
   For the high, sun-ligh-ted win-dows co-lored or clear.

2. Some de-light in coun-try cha-pel built on a hill;
   O-thers kneel in great ca-the-dral, dim lit and still;
   Tem-ple con-gre-ga-tions sing the Psalms loved of yore:
   All are set a-part for wor-ship, God to a-dore.

No matter how different are the houses and the ways of worship, the same God is worshiped in all of the places.

Music copyrighted 1920 by The St. Gregory Guild, Inc. *By permission of The St. Gregory Guild, Inc., Philadelphia, Pennsylvania.*

GOD OF ALL

Translated from the Hebrew
by S. Dinin

El Kabir
Jewish Folk Song

With dignity

1. God of all, we sing your praises; You have been our people's might; Lend us strength to live and la-bor, Seek for truth and work for right.
2. Migh-ty God, pro-tect your chil-dren When they cry in sore di-stress; Give to us your boun-teous bles-sing, Grant us peace and hap-pi-ness.

Adapted from *Songs of Zion*, compiled and edited by Harry Coopersmith,
Behrman House, Inc., Publishers, New York.

THIS IS MY FATHER'S WORLD

Maltbie D. Babcock Franklin L. Sheppard

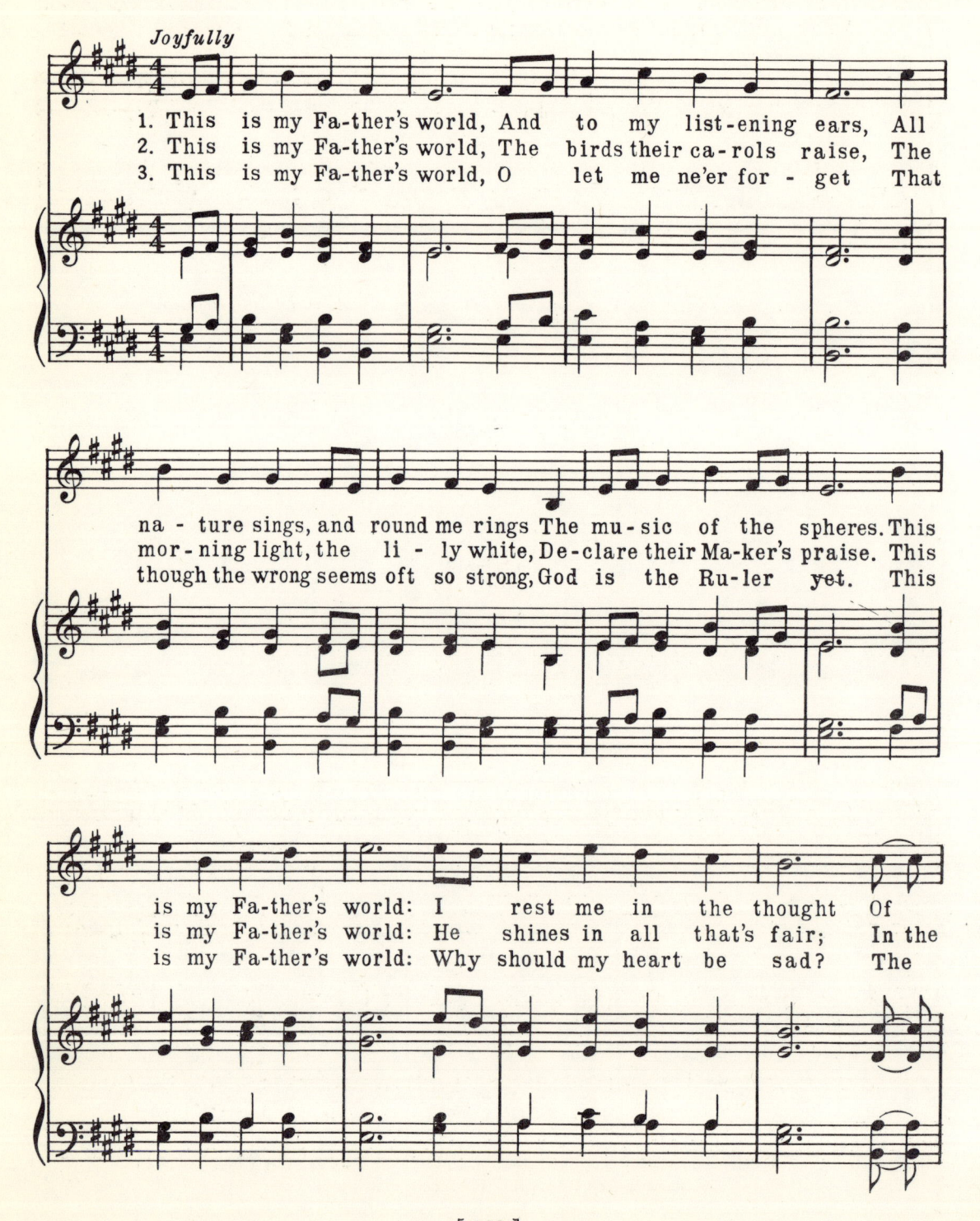

Joyfully

1. This is my Fa-ther's world, And to my list-ening ears, All na-ture sings, and round me rings The mu-sic of the spheres. This is my Fa-ther's world: I rest me in the thought Of
2. This is my Fa-ther's world, The birds their ca-rols raise, The morn-ing light, the li-ly white, De-clare their Ma-ker's praise. This is my Fa-ther's world: He shines in all that's fair; In the
3. This is my Fa-ther's world, O let me ne'er for-get That though the wrong seems oft so strong, God is the Ru-ler yet. This is my Fa-ther's world: Why should my heart be sad? The

rocks and trees, of skies and seas; His hand the won-ders wrought.
rust-ling grass I hear him pass, He speaks to me eve-ry-where.
Lord is King: let the hea-vens ring! God reigns: let the earth be glad!

Words reprinted from *Thoughts for Everyday Living*, by Maltbie D. Babcock; copyright 1901 by Charles Scribner's Sons, 1929 by Katharine T. Babcock; *used by permission of the publishers.*

A THANKFUL SONG

Mary Rumsey   Alsatian

Moderato

To God, who gives our dai-ly bread, A thank-ful song we'll raise,

And pray that he, who sends us food, May fill our hearts with praise.

[109]

STORIES OF JESUS

William H. Parker Frederic A. Challinor

Brightly, not too fast

1. Tell me the sto-ries of Je-sus I love to hear;
2. First let me hear how the chil-dren Stood round his knee;
3. In-to the ci-ty I'd fol-low The chil-dren's band,

Things I would ask him to tell me If he were here;
And I shall fan-cy his bles-sing Re-sting on me;
Wa-ving a branch of a palm tree High in my hand;

Scenes by the way-side, Tales of the sea,
Words full of kind-ness, Deeds full of grace,
One of his he-ralds, Yes, I would sing

Sto-ries of Je-sus, Tell them to me.
All in the love-light Of Je-sus' face.
Lou-dest ho-san-nas! Je-sus is King!

By permission of the National Sunday School Union.

GOOD NEWS

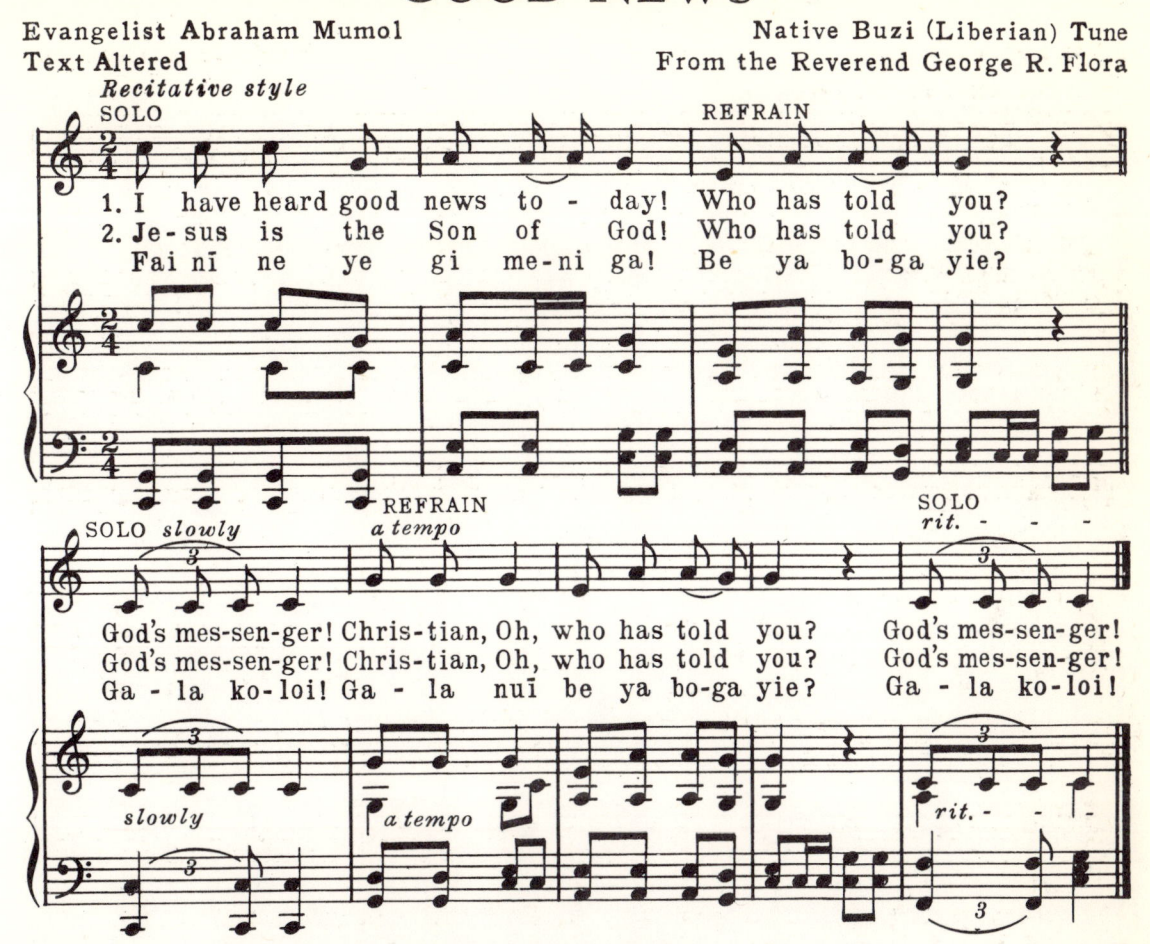

Evangelist Abraham Mumol
Text Altered

Native Buzi (Liberian) Tune
From the Reverend George R. Flora

Recitative style

1. I have heard good news to-day! Who has told you? God's mes-sen-ger! Chris-tian, Oh, who has told you? God's mes-sen-ger!
2. Je-sus is the Son of God! Who has told you? God's mes-sen-ger! Chris-tian, Oh, who has told you? God's mes-sen-ger!

Fai nī ne ye gi me-ni ga! Be ya bo-ga yie? Ga - la ko-loi! Ga - la nuī be ya bo-ga yie? Ga - la ko-loi!

3. SOLO: Jesus is the friend of all!
   REFRAIN: Who has told you?
   SOLO: God's messenger!
   REFRAIN: Christian, Oh, who has told you?
   SOLO: God's messenger!

This song shows how local customs are adapted to Christian uses. One day a missionary, Mr. Flora, was visiting Evangelist Abraham Mumol in Fissibon, when he heard the children singing, clapping their hands, and stamping their feet to mark the rhythm. He learned that they were using the music of a folk song to which had been set the words given above. Drums and rattles are used as the natives sing. All consonants are harsh. Short *i* as in *knit*; short *e* as in *get*; long *i* as *ee*; *y* is soft guttural, like *gh* in *sigh*; diphthong *ai* as *eye*; *oi* as in *boy*.

Printed by permission of the Women's Missionary Society of the United Lutheran Church in America.

PRAYER FOR AIRMEN

Harry Webb Farrington

Byrd
Rob Roy Peery

Forcefully

1. O God Creator, in whose hand The rolling planets lie, Give skill to those who now command The ships that brave the sky.
2. Strong Spirit, burning with mankind On missions high to dare, Safe pilot all who seek to find Their haven through the air.
3. Enfolding Life, bear on thy wing Through storm, and dark, and sun, The men in air who closer bring The nations into one.

Words copyright, 1928, by Harry Webb Farrington. *Used by permission of Mrs. Farrington.*
Music copyright, 1929, by Rob Roy Peery. *Used by permission.*

OUR HOLY GUEST

Henry van Dyke
Prayerfully
"FAITH" MOTIVE

Motives from *Parsifal*
Richard Wagner

Lord Jesus, be our holy Guest, Our morning joy, our evening rest; And with our daily bread impart Thy love and peace to every heart.

"HOLY GRAIL" MOTIVE (DRESDEN AMEN)

A - men, A - men.

Words from *The Book of Common Worship*, copyright, 1932, by the Presbyterian Board of Christian Education. *Used by permission.*

FAR AWAY IN OLD JUDEA

Walter J. Mathams Carey Bonner

1. Far away in old Judea, Lived the gentle Lord of love; Happy children gathered round him, Wheresoever he might move, And they sometimes left their play, Just to follow him all day.
2. Through the fields he often led them, Where the lovely lilies grew, Where the crested lark went singing Upward to the sky so blue; Thus with him and birds and flowers, Glad they spent the golden hours.
3. Wondrous stories Jesus told them Of our Father's thoughtful care; How he loves us, leads us, keeps us, Every day and everywhere; So we never need to fear, Since his help is always near.

Words adapted from *Song and Play for Children*, by Danielson and Conant. Copyright, The Pilgrim Press. *Used by permission.*

SPLENDID ARE THE HEAVENS

N. F. S. Grundtvig
In stately movement
Danish

1. Splen-did are the hea-vens high, Beau-ti-ful the ra-diant sky,
2. It was on the ho-ly night. Dark-ness veiled the stars so bright;
3. Sa-ges from the East a-far, When they saw this won-drous star,

Where the gol-den stars are shi-ning, And their rays to earth in-cli-ning,
But at once the hea-vens hoa-ry Were be-decked with light and glo-ry,
Went to find this King of na-tions, And to of-fer their o-bla-tions

Beck'-ning us to heaven a-bove, Beck'-ning us to heaven a-bove.
Co-ming from a won-drous star, Co-ming from a won-drous star.
Un-to him as Lord and King, Un-to him as Lord and King.

All through the centuries men have wondered how the Lord of the universe could be concerned with human beings. The psalmist said, "... as I look up to the heavens thy fingers made, ... I ask, 'And what is man, that thou should'st think of him?'"

From *Carols, Customs and Costumes around the World*, compiled by Herbert H. Wernecke.
By permission of The Old Orchard Publishers, Webster Groves, Missouri.

MANITOU LISTENS TO ME

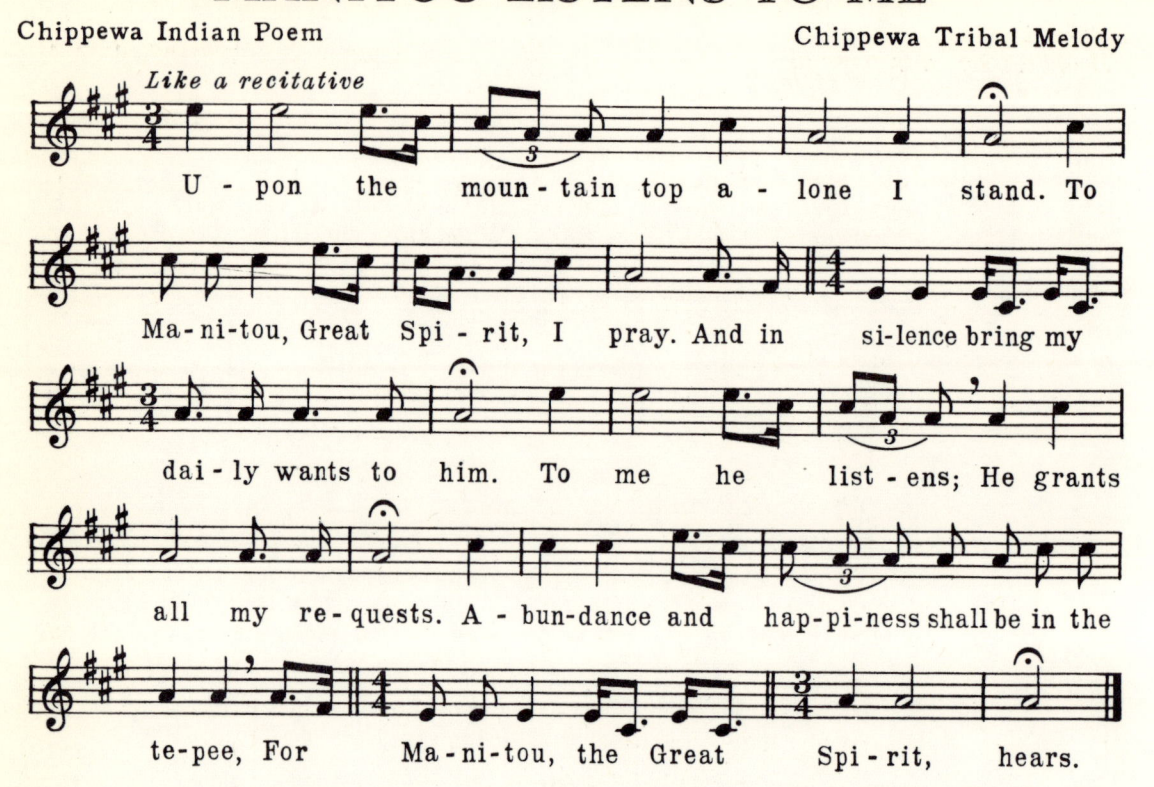

Chippewa Indian Poem
Chippewa Tribal Melody

Like a recitative

U-pon the moun-tain top a-lone I stand. To Ma-ni-tou, Great Spi-rit, I pray. And in si-lence bring my dai-ly wants to him. To me he list-ens; He grants all my re-quests. A-bun-dance and hap-pi-ness shall be in the te-pee, For Ma-ni-tou, the Great Spi-rit, hears.

The Indian cultivates habits of silence, thoughtfulness, and communion with the Spirit of Life. *Manitou* means "Master of Life"; a *tepee* is a cone-shaped tent in which the Indian lives.

From *Bureau of American Ethnology Bulletin 45.* Used by permission of the Bureau of American Ethnology, Washington, D. C.

HOLY, HOLY, HOLY

Based on *Isaiah 6: 3*
"Seymour," Abridged
Carl M. von Weber, 1826

Reverently

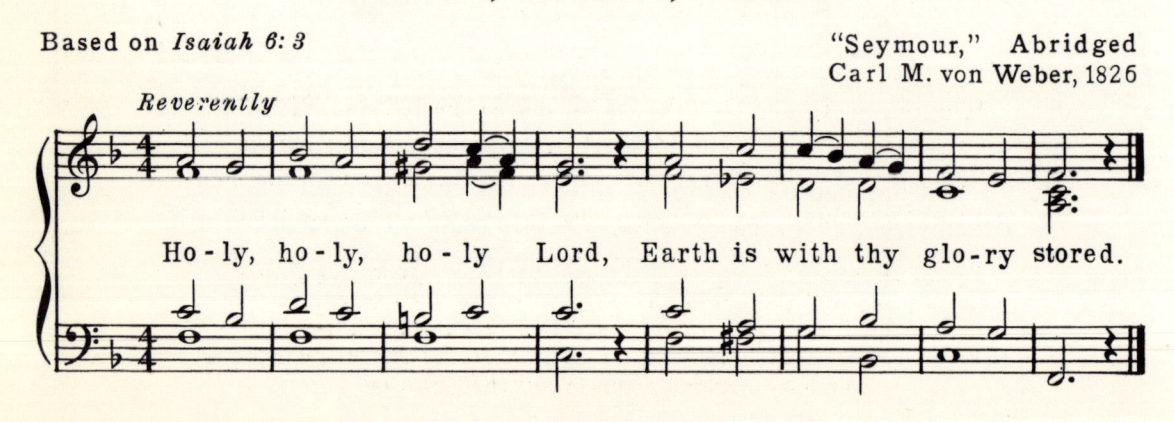

Ho-ly, ho-ly, ho-ly Lord, Earth is with thy glo-ry stored.

PRAYER FOR SCHOOLBOYS

Indian Lyric
Translated by M. K. Gandhi

Fragment of a Hindustani Air

ONE VOICE: In the name of God.
May he protect us.
May he support us.

RESPONSE BY GROUP

Slowly, solemnly

In the name of God, Peace.

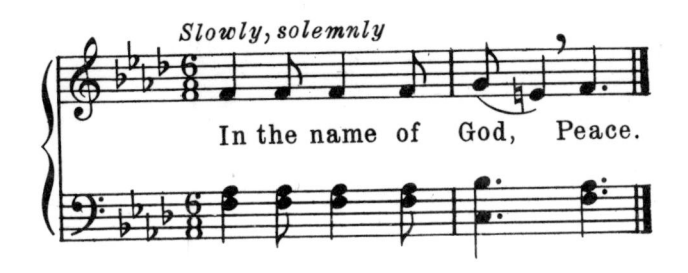

ONE VOICE: May we go forward together,
True comrades.
May our search after truth find its fruit.

RESPONSE BY GROUP   (as above)

ONE VOICE: May we never hold in our hearts
Ill-will the one for the other.

RESPONSE BY GROUP   (as above)

    This prayer, translated from an Indian lyric by Mahatma Gandhi, is for the use of boys in a "Youth Place of Worship" ("Kumar Mandir"). A haunting air from Hindustan accompanies the response. The ideas expressed on sharing bring Eastern and Western schoolboys together.

Words from *Songs from Prison*, translation of Indian lyrics, by M. K. Gandhi, adapted for the press by John S. Hoyland. *By permission of The Macmillan Company, publishers, New York, and George Allen & Unwin Ltd., London.*
Music adapted from *"Oriental Miscellany,"* by William Hamilton Bird, *"Airs of Hindoostan,"* Calcutta, Joseph Cooper, 1789.

THE COMPANY OF JESUS

Edith Lovell Thomas   J. S. Bach, 1736

Eagerly

1. The simple fishermen Cast nets into the sea,
And Jesus watched them, as he walked Beside Lake Galilee;
He called; they rowed ashore; With joy they made the choice

2. New trails they broke with him Through fields, up mountainside;
They cared for sick and hungry ones, In training with their Guide.
Real comrades they became, Less fearful and more brave,

3. They shared his daring dreams: His hope that every one
Would carry on, with Jesus' help, The work he had begun.
His circle, once so small, Now 'round the earth extends,

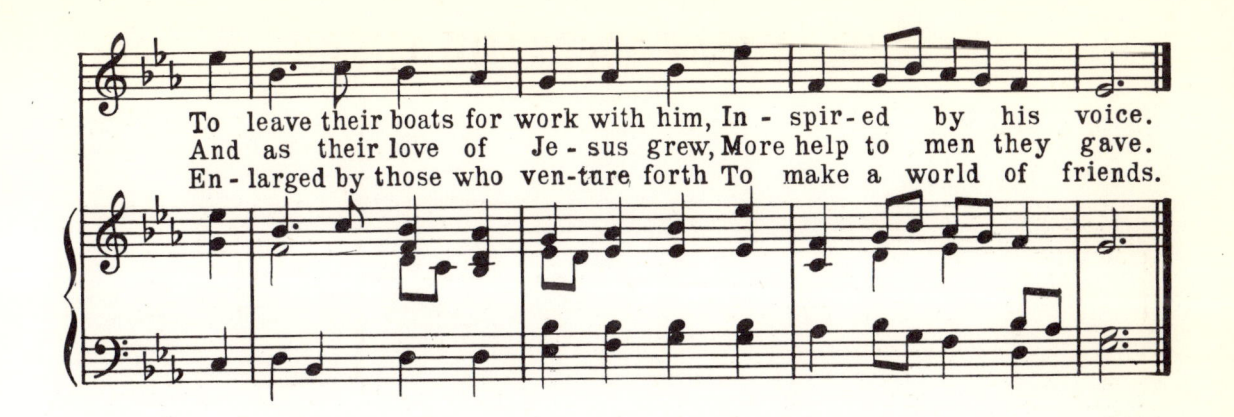

To leave their boats for work with him, In - spir - ed by his voice.
And as their love of Je - sus grew, More help to men they gave.
En - larged by those who ven - ture forth To make a world of friends.

The Bach Chorale takes in every note of the scale and one above for good measure, in its up-and-down journey, and suggests the story of the travels of Jesus with his twelve disciples in Palestine.

LOVELY APPEAR

Based on *Isaiah 52:7*

From *The Redemption*
Charles Gounod

Moderato

p Love - ly ap - pear o - ver the moun - tains The feet of them that preach, and bring good news of peace, The feet of them that preach, and bring good news of peace.

[119]

ONE FATHER

Based on the Bible
Edith Lovell Thomas

Arranged from Siegfried Ochs

Not too slowly

1. Have we not all One Father, God? Has not one God Cre-a-ted us One fa-mi-ly Daugh-ters and sons?
2. Fa - - - ther of all, To thee we sing, To thee we pray Chil-dren of thine, Drawn by thy love, We wor-ship thee!

THANK THEE, GOD

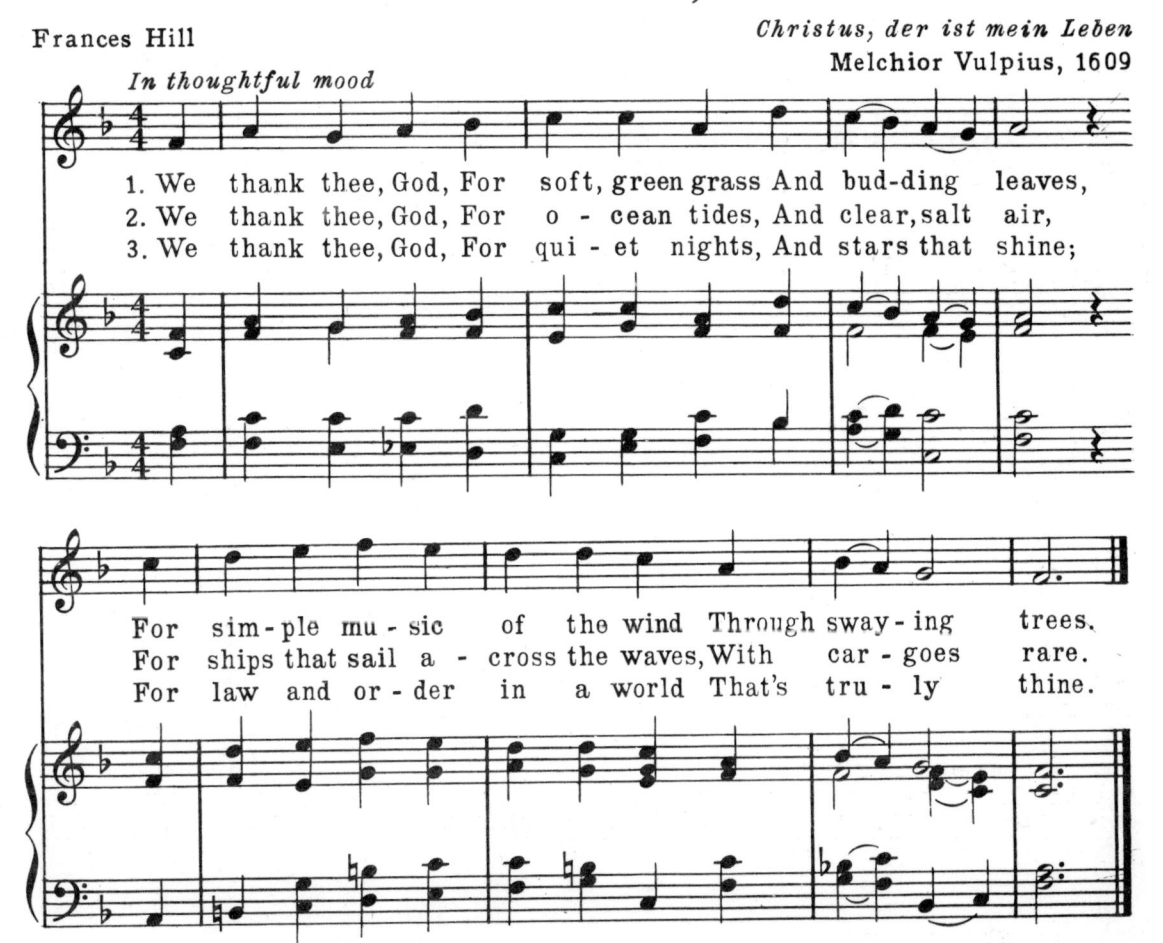

Frances Hill

Christus, der ist mein Leben
Melchior Vulpius, 1609

In thoughtful mood

1. We thank thee, God, For soft, green grass And bud-ding leaves,
   For sim-ple mu-sic of the wind Through sway-ing trees.
2. We thank thee, God, For o-cean tides, And clear, salt air,
   For ships that sail a-cross the waves, With car-goes rare.
3. We thank thee, God, For qui-et nights, And stars that shine;
   For law and or-der in a world That's tru-ly thine.

4. We thank thee, God,
   For thoughts of men,
   And deeds of worth;
   For those whose lives and love reveal
   Thy will on earth.

Words used by permission of the author

HYMN OF PRAISE

The High Road of Song
Franz Schubert
Abridged

Allegretto

1. The sun shines in splen-dor, and blue is the sky, The birds are all sing-ing with joy as they fly; The ri-vers are win-ding be-tween woo-ded shores; The whole world of na-ture its Ma-ker a-dores.
2. The bil-lows of o-cean are soun-ding his praise, Who li-veth for-e - ver, the An-cient of Days; The moun-tains their sum-mits lift up to the sky, His al-tars, who reign-eth e-ter-nal on high.
3. Then lift up your voi-ces, you chil-dren of men, Your hearts lift in an-thems of wor-ship a-gain; For we, too, will praise him, the Fa-ther of love, Who sen-deth his power and his grace from a-bove.

From *The High Road of Song*, by Robert Foresman. *By permission of the publishers,*
American Book Company, New York.

INDEX BY COUNTRIES

(The songs are grouped according to the countries from which the music comes.)

AFRICAN
A Christmas Antiphon (South Africa) . 93
A-Fishing (Gold Coast) 24
Before Dinner (Congo) 26
Congo Lullaby (Congo) 63
Good News (Liberia) 111
Seeds We Bring (Portuguese East Africa) . 30
The Magic Tom-Tom (Congo) 51

ALSATIAN
A Prayer of Thanks 58
A Thankful Song 109
Doing Nothing But Sing 13
Praise and Thanksgiving 103
The Christ Child's Stable 92

AMERICAN
A Thanksgiving 80
Back of the Bread 77
Before Worship 103
Friendship Song 45
Let All the World 12
Mighty Day (Negro Spiritual) . . . 86
What Is Peace 52
Pippa's Song 72
Prayer for Airmen 112
Sounds That Make Us Glad 71
Study War No More (Negro Spiritual) . 53
This Is My Father's World 108

AMERICAN INDIAN
Making Maple Sugar (Chippewa) . . . 28
Manitou Listens to Me (Chippewa) . . 116

ARMENIAN
Lullaby to the Christ Child 88

AUSTRIAN
Hymn of Praise 122

BELGIAN
O Praise Ye the Lord 105

BRAZILIAN
Thanks to God 18

CHINESE
Chinese Lullaby 60
Fat Baby Sister 61
High Is the Blue Sky 76
Oath of Friendship 54
Yangtze Boatmen's Chantey 29

CROATIAN
Firefly 74

CZECHOSLOVAKIAN
Ploughing 38

DANISH
Splendid Are the Heavens 115

ENGLISH
Chums 47
Come Out to Play 13
Far Away in Old Judea 114
From Every Land 42
Partners 82
St. Valentine's Day 98
Stories of Jesus 110
The First Courier 98

FILIPINO
Planting Rice 22

FINNISH
Workers Together 21

FRENCH
A Joyful Thing 86
Fellowship of Song 11
Houses of Worship 106
Lovely Appear 119
Round of the Oats 23
What Do We Plant 78

GERMAN
All Glory, Laud, and Honor 100
Easter Surprises 70
From Heaven High 90
Holy, Holy, Holy 116
Merry Christmas 85
One Father 120
Our Beautiful Earth 41
Our Holy Guest 113
Round the World 44
Thank Thee, God 121
The Company of Jesus 118
The Piper 16

GREEK
Shiny Little Moon 74

GUATEMALAN
The Carpenter 27

HAWAIIAN
With Needle and Thread 35

INDIAN
Balloon Song (Marathi) 62
Fruits and Vegetables (Marathi) . . . 31
Prayer for Schoolboys (Hindustan) . . . 117
Shawl Weaver's Song (Cashmere) . . . 34

IRISH
For Children 69

ITALIAN
Canticle to the Sun 14

JAPANESE
Birthday Presents 96
Mary's Lullaby 91
My Doll 64

JEWISH
Chanukah 97

God of All 107
Tramping 48

KOREAN
Bright Moon 75

MEXICAN
Christmas in Mexico 94, 95

NEW ZEALAND
Canoe Song 50

PERUVIAN
Sung at Harvest Time 32

POLISH
God's World 57

PUERTO RICAN
The Little Jesus 89

RUSSIAN
A Russian Landscape 49

SAMOAN
Samoa 59
With Needle and Thread 35

SWEDISH
My Homeland 65

SWISS
All People 104
Through Every Land 104

TYROLESE
Calling the Cows 36

URUGUAYAN
Every Small Inch of Farm Land 25

WELSH
Hail, Guest 46

INDEX OF FIRST LINES AND TITLES

(Titles appear in capitals)

A CHRISTMAS ANTIPHON	93
A happy New Year	81
A JOYFUL THING	86
A little light is going by	74
A PRAYER OF THANKS	58
A RUSSIAN LANDSCAPE	49
A THANKFUL SONG	109
A THANKSGIVING	80
A-FISHING	24
All children who live in distant lands	45
All glory, laud, and honor	100
ALL PEOPLE	104
All people that on earth do dwell	104
All the world is God's world	57
BACK OF THE BREAD	77
Back of the bread is the snowy flour	77
BALLOON SONG	62
BEFORE DINNER	26
BEFORE WORSHIP	103
BIRTHDAY PRESENTS	96
Boom, boom, boom, boom, boom	51
BRIGHT MOON	75
Buy vegetables	31
CALLING THE COWS	36
CANOE SONG	50
CANTICLE TO THE SUN	14
CHANUKAH	97
Chanukah, Chanukah	97
CHINESE LULLABY	60
CHRISTMAS IN MEXICO	94, 95
CHUMS	47
Come and see	75
Come, my sisters, come, my brothers	32
COME OUT TO PLAY	13
Come, shepherds, come to Bethlehem today	89
CONGO LULLABY	63
Cup of warm milk	96
Deftly, deftly, nimble fingers	34
DOING NOTHING BUT SING	13
EASTER SURPRISES	70
Every small inch of farm land	25
Far away in old Judea	114
FAT BABY SISTER	61
FELLOWSHIP OF SONG	11
FIREFLY	74
First we go to hoe our garden	26
FOR CHILDREN	69
For summer rain and winter's sun	80
FRIENDSHIP SONG	45
From all that dwell below the skies	104
FROM EVERY LAND	42
FROM HEAVEN HIGH	90
From heaven high I come to earth	90
FRUITS AND VEGETABLES	31
Girls and boys, come out to play	13
Gladly to the house of worship	106
GOD OF ALL	107
God of all, we sing your praises	107
GOD'S WORLD	57
Goin' to lay down my sword and shield	53
GOOD NEWS	111
Hail, Guest	46
HAPPY NEW YEAR	81
Hark to the cowherd's merry calling	36
Have we not all one Father, God	120
High and blue the sky	76
HIGH IS THE BLUE SKY	76
HOLY, HOLY, HOLY	116
Holy, holy, holy Lord	116
HOUSES OF WORSHIP	106
How beautiful is the green earth	41
HYMN OF PRAISE	122
I had a willow whistle	16
I have heard good news today	111
I love God's tiny creatures	69
I want to be your friend	54
I'd love to be a shepherd boy tonight	98
In the morning when I waken	18
In the name of God, Peace	117
In the name of merciful heaven	94
Jesus Christ was born on Christmas	93
LET ALL THE WORLD	12
Let all the world in every corner sing	12
Let the doors fly open wide	95
Let us go to the sugar camp	28
Lord Jesus, be our holy Guest	113
LOVELY APPEAR	119
Lovely appear over the mountains	119
LULLABY TO THE CHRIST CHILD	88

MAKING MAPLE SUGAR	28
MANITOU LISTENS TO ME	116
MARY'S LULLABY	91
MERRY CHRISTMAS	85
MIGHTY DAY	86
Mwana, dear, now do not cry . . .	63
My country is the world	66
MY DOLL	64
MY HOMELAND	65
My house has a fat baby wee . . .	61
Ning-yo, you're a lovely doll . . .	64
Now up and now down glides our canoe .	50
O Father, thou who givest all . . .	58
O God Creator, in whose hand . . .	112
O God, thy rain and sun and soil . .	21
O Lord, we praise thee for our Brother Sun	14
O praise ye the Lord	105
OATH OF FRIENDSHIP	54
On the hay in the stable	91
ONE FATHER	120
OUR BEAUTIFUL EARTH	41
OUR HOLY GUEST	113
Our thoughts go round the world . . .	44
Out of an egg comes a singing bird . . .	70
PARTNERS	82
Peace is God's blessing upon the world .	52
PIPPA'S SONG	72
PLANTING RICE	22
Planting rice is never fun	22
PLOUGHING	38
PRAISE AND THANKSGIVING . .	103
Praise and thanksgiving let everyone bring	103
PRAYER FOR AIRMEN	112
PRAYER FOR SCHOOLBOYS . . .	117
Rainbows in the sky	59
River boatmen we	29
ROUND OF THE OATS	23
ROUND THE WORLD	44
ST. VALENTINE'S DAY	98
SAMOA	59
See, Oh, see our charming balloon . .	62
Seeds we bring	30
SHAWL WEAVER'S SONG . . .	34
SHINY LITTLE MOON	74
Shiny little moon, tonight	74
Sleep, my baby, my beloved	88
SOUNDS THAT MAKE US GLAD . .	71
SPLENDID ARE THE HEAVENS . .	115
Splendid are the heavens high . . .	115
STORIES OF JESUS	110

STUDY WAR NO MORE	53
SUNG AT HARVEST TIME . . .	32
Tell me the stories of Jesus	110
THANK THEE, GOD	121
THANKS TO GOD	18
THE CARPENTER	27
THE CHRIST CHILD'S STABLE . .	92
THE COMPANY OF JESUS . . .	118
THE FIRST COURIER	98
THE LITTLE JESUS	89
THE MAGIC TOM-TOM	51
THE PIPER	16
The simple fishermen	118
The stable was old and rude . . .	92
The sun shines in splendor	122
The world came to my home today . .	42
The year's at the spring	72
This is my Father's world	108
Thou hast put gladness in my heart . .	71
THROUGH EVERY LAND	104
Through the forest blows the tempest .	49
To God, who gives our daily bread . .	109
Tomorrow is St. Valentine's Day . .	98
TRAMPING	48
Upon the mountain top alone I stand . .	116
Walk slowly	103
Wasn't that a mighty day	86
We come, we come	24
We have tomorrow	17
We long to go to the homeland . . .	65
We thank thee, God	121
We're off to the forest	48
We've been told a joyful thing . . .	86
WHAT DO WE PLANT	78
What do we plant when we plant a tree .	78
WHAT IS PEACE	52
When your voice with every other's . .	11
Where will you go	38
Who digs a well, or plants a seed . . .	82
Who wants to hear, who wants to know .	23
Who would desire a pleasanter thing . .	13
Willows are bending and murmuring low .	60
With his saw the honest carpenter . . .	27
WITH NEEDLE AND THREAD . .	35
With needle and thread and flowers . .	35
WORKERS TOGETHER	21
YANGTZE BOATMEN'S CHANTEY .	29
Yes, Christmas is coming	85
You see, we three	47
YOUTH	17

A NOTE ABOUT THE BOOK

The text in this book
is set in Linotype Garamond ✻
Music and text notes printed by
Robert Teller Sons & Dorner ✻ Special
matter and display type set by The Composing Room ✻ Bound in paper by Tauber's
Bookbindery, Inc., in cloth by Charles
H. Bohn & Company ✻ The paper is
Beckett Offset India ✻ The cloths
are Columbia Lynbrook 451 and
Bancroft Natural Finish,
Sky Gray.

New York 1950